Hitting the Innovation
Jackpot

Practical Essays on Innovation

Dr. Darren McKnight

iUniverse, Inc.
Bloomington

iUniverse books may be ordered through booksellers or by contacting:

iUniverse
1663 Liberty Drive
Bloomington, IN 47403
www.iuniverse.com
1-800-Authors (1-800-288-4677)

ISBN: 978-1-4620-7010-7 (sc)
ISBN: 978-1-4620-7011-4 (hc)
ISBN: 978-1-4620-7012-1 (e)

Library of Congress Control Number: 2011961815

Printed in the United States of America

iUniverse rev. date: 12/01/2011

Contents

Foreword

This book can change your life by influencing your mind-set. The results we enjoy in life are dependent on the beliefs we hold, not merely on the behaviors we display. Dr. Darren McKnight supports the premise that a clear vision, followed by a solid strategy that is focused on consistent execution, wins the day—every time. He's right. Doesn't sound much like innovation, does it?

Well, by dissecting the core principles of innovation and building them back up piece by piece in this series of essays, Darren crafts a story that is compelling in its simplicity. Yet, as the author highlights, simple is not easy; so the practical examples throughout the book provide sparks of insight that you will be able to apply immediately.

Creativity is about doing things differently. Innovation is about doing things better. That's what this work is all about. You can always be better; you just have to have the courage to make the effort. This book provides an ample supply of information, knowledge, and wisdom that can guide you, your team, and your organization through the journey of discovery.

More importantly, this book provides a guide as to how you innovate. If someone tells you what to do to solve a problem quickly and effectively, that will help you once. Being a pragmatic visionary means that you have combined the passion and vision of an artist with the precision and focus of an engineer. The result is the flexibility and confidence to handle any challenge, anytime.

Darren's success in a wide range of technical and professional venues accentuates his unique perspective on the establishment and execution of innovation practices. He has truly "been there and done that."

The ideas discussed in these pages make a lot of sense. I know. In 2005 I became president of a small university in High Point, North Carolina, with only 375 freshmen and a total undergraduate population of 1,450 students. We were a landlocked institution in the middle of a residential area in the center of the city. Few thought High Point University would ever be noticed on the national scene.

They were wrong. Today, High Point University is a thriving academy with 1,400 freshmen and 4,000 undergraduates. It is ranked among the top colleges in the South and employs innovative concepts and principles to ensure that every student receives an extraordinary education in an inspiring environment with caring people. We brought together a diverse team, identified challenging goals, looked each other in the eye, and built on the trust that we would be an extraordinary university. The rest is history! All of this only proves that what Darren McKnight talks about is pragmatic and functional—in any setting.

Dr. Nido R. Qubein, president, High Point University

Preface

I love my job! Most people cannot say that because they are busy trying to solve other people's problems or live up to other people's expectations. I learned a long time ago to be proactive and plan for success by being the very best at whatever I do. When I went to the United States Air Force Academy, I was challenged to the limits of my abilities and energy but found a special strength in the teamwork-oriented military. Our squadron won the award for the top organization an unprecedented three years in a row. That had never happened before. I think it was at that early stage that the genesis for this book was laid. I saw people from all backgrounds coming together to tackle challenges that none of us ever imagined we could tackle. So I started paying attention to what worked and what did not work.

In my first assignment in the air force, I was tasked with operating and improving fiber-optic data acquisition systems used in the simulation of nuclear-weapons effects on strategic military systems. I had never even heard of fiber optics before I arrived at my base, but within one year I had been recognized as the top performer out of ten thousand professionals for my technical accomplishments. At this point, I started to crystallize the concept that it is not so important *what* you do, but rather *how* you do it. I did a lot right while I was there; but believe me, I also made mistakes. I wrote those mistakes down and have thought about them over the years. It is okay to make a mistake; but, like the old saying tells us, "Never make the same mistake twice."

The air force offered to send me back to school, so I thought that I would continue to broaden my horizons and decided to pursue a PhD in aerospace engineering sciences at the University of Colorado (CU). When I contacted my advisor he offered up a technically challenging concept of modeling orbital pellet swarms. While an academically intriguing area, I did not see the value to the aerospace community. As a result, I researched real-world applications and determined that the burgeoning field of artificial space debris was a relevant application of the concepts my advisor wanted me to tackle. With a value proposition for my endeavors and the support of several colleagues in the arena, I not only finished my doctoral program in two and a half years but also established a funded research program at CU and coauthored the first book ever on orbital debris. My success was borne out of basic tenets that I discuss in this book: listen, learn, and write things down.

I left the air force and continued to address critical national and international issues related to the space debris environment. I worked on several multinational, multidisciplinary teams that unearthed significant insights into the growing hazard from orbital debris. During this time, I learned to appreciate the same cognitive diversity of teams that powered my early success at the Air Force Academy and found it to be equally important in international fora.

While many people who receive their doctorates feel that they have become experts and that it is time for others to listen to them, my approach was quite to the contrary. I knew that now was the time to pay attention to successful people and organizations around me so I could continue to document the basics of success and innovation.

My industry career provided the opportunity to work for a company with a diverse set of technologies that I was responsible for applying to customer needs. I had expanded my modeling and simulation capabilities of the space environment into the terrestrial battlefield arena. I was asked to help address the most difficult of all problems at the time: the inclusion of chemical and biological agent transport, dispersion, and effects in virtual reality simulations. During this intensive period of research and development (R&D) I noted an interesting dilemma. If chemical or biological agents were used against our soldiers, marines, or airmen we had very few options as to how we could decontaminate the soiled material from such encounters. At the same time, our company had a commercial capability to eradicate biological pathogens such as *E. coli* and salmonella in poultry and hamburger meat. Oh, well. This was just an interesting combination of technologies, right? Wrong!

I proposed to the US Army that the same device that we used to make a rare hamburger safe to eat (by killing the *E. coli* bacteria) might also be used to decontaminate material exposed to biological agents. After an extensive testing program, the technical results were presented in 2001 six months before the buildings in Washington, DC, were contaminated with the *bacillus anthracis* spores. Our solution for cleaning up the tons of soiled mail was the only approach available to our government. I was very busy for two years and even traveled internationally representing new mail-security approaches. How did an aerospace engineer craft a unique solution to a first-ever health disaster? I applied the fundamental innovation principles that I have outlined in this book.

I had been coaching my daughters' soccer teams for years despite my lack of formal training or experience in playing soccer. I read many soccer coaching books, looking for help in what I needed most—trying to get a swarm of girls on the soccer field to move down the field with purpose and still have fun! Unfortunately, all of the coaching books were just a series of drills focused on specific situations and were not designed for players easily distracted by butterflies; clearly not useful for me as I was trying to get eight-year-old girls to work together. So, being "brilliant in my ignorance," I came up with my own techniques to coach youth soccer. As these techniques evolved, people would say to me, "I have never seen that before," and I thought that it was probably time to write down everything and make it available to other people.

The book evolved over several years of my coaching, especially with the assistance of a real soccer trainer, Radovan Pletka. I was incrementally aggressive about documenting and applying innovation fundamentals to soccer that I had noted and used in my business career. The result is an excellent book about youth soccer coaching called *Soccer is a Thinking Game* that provides the counterintuitive advice that, for a coach, "what you do off the field is more important than what you do on the field" and that, for players, "what you do without the ball is more important than what you do with the ball." My youngest daughter is now playing high school soccer and these axioms, borne of desperation by an engineer coaching soccer, still hold true today.

As my work and the world have gotten more high tech, I have worked hard to maintain balance in my personal and business life by clinging to high-touch (i.e., personal) rituals. During my career, I have tried to be a careful historian of events developing before me. This introspection has served me well. I have also focused on the personal side of innovation, resisting the appeal of having a thousand "friends" on Facebook. My focus has been on having dozens of friends that I meet with regularly over coffee or a stack of pancakes to discuss our successes and failures.

From this group of successful innovators, I have drawn in a group to provide guest essays for this book. The authors—scientist, corporate strategist, musician, chief executive officer, intelligence analyst, political strategist, program manager, coach, trainer, and consultant—were selected to cover a wide enough swath of careers to reinforce the utility of innovative principles in any facet of life. The guest essays appear at the end of the book and provide a means to cement the thesis of this book and highlight valuable universal innovation fundamentals. It is fascinating how this diverse group of individuals has so much in common. These essays provide practical examples of implementing innovative processes in a wide variety of domains, plus many amusing, thought-provoking, and relevant anecdotes.

Acknowledgments

I would like to thank all of my colleagues and friends who have put their time and energy into the countless coffeehouse chats, technical sidebar discussions, and intellectual dialogues over breakfast. Your words and insights have inspired me to document the choicest of our joint musings. A special thanks is extended to Frank Di Pentino, who pushed me to keep going at that awkward midpoint of writing this book and, in concert with Waseem Haider, helped me to craft the title of this book.

This book was an experiment in itself, as I have asked individuals from a very diverse range of communities, backgrounds, and demographics to each contribute a guest innovation essay. I was amazed and humbled by the richness and acuity of these stories. Thanks to all of the guest authors for taking their "homework assignment" so seriously and contributing markedly to the value of *Hitting the Innovation Jackpot*.

I greatly appreciate the support of Dr. Nido Qubein for this book. High Point University (HPU) is truly a place that has hit the innovation jackpot. HPU is a rare institution that encourages its students to be extraordinary in all aspects of their lives.

My current employer, Integrity Applications Incorporated (IAI), has provided a wonderful platform for me to hone my innovation practice. IAI provides a fertile infrastructure for exploring and solving many of our nation's most challenging problems. Our recognition By the Great Place to Work Institute in 2011 as the second-best medium-sized company to work for in America accentuates IAI's commitment to providing a quality workplace for all of our employees.

This book is dedicated to the three ladies in my life: Alison, Olivia, and Grace. Their love, humor, and encouragement over the years have been driving forces in my life. Thanks for being there for me.

About the Front Cover

Don't let the success of your company be left to chance. *Hitting the Innovation Jackpot* takes the mystery and risk out of realizing true value from innovation initiatives that include all strata of the enterprise: individuals, teams, and the organization.

About Back Cover

The back cover shows two HPU students (Olivia McKnight and Dushante Davis) flanking a statue of Galileo Galelei, one of the most innovative astronomers the world has ever known. This contrast of the past and the future on one of the most enlightened campuses in America provides a compelling backdrop to *Hitting the Innovation Jackpot*. They dare you to be extraordinary! (Photograph by James (Chad) Christian from HPU.)

Introduction

There are so many innovation books being written, published, and read. Many of these books are good; however, many are not. The primary concern that I have as I have consumed many of these books is that all of the good ones are basically saying the same thing. However, the common facets of innovation are not apparent in these books since each normally takes the form of a case study where a specific implementation for a specific industry is detailed. The hidden, fundamental innovation principles are the ones I will focus on in this book.

These fundamentals are the "blocking and tackling" of innovation, which begin with the simple question: What is innovation? Is it creative problem solving, user-centered design, workforce productivity, or all of the above? Innovation is not only difficult to inspire, plan, and execute, but for some it is actually even difficult to define.

In John Denver's popular song "Perhaps Love," he captured many of the same fleeting feelings about innovation that many grapple with in describing love. The following lines are especially relevant in our determining how we are going to consider innovation.

"For some a way of living, for some a way to feel "

For some, innovation is a way of living that is so engrained that it is impossible to separate applying innovation techniques from just doing business. However, many just *feel* innovation. The term *innovative culture* is always distracting since it implies subjective feelings, and it is difficult to pin down specific actions or behavior. Yet the actions and behaviors at multiple levels will be emphasized in this book as the only ways to make an organization more innovative.

"And some say love is holding on, and some say letting go "

Many organizations, teams, and individuals deal with the difficult quandary of whether innovation comes from what they know best or if it comes from starting over with all new people, processes, and technologies. Clearly, there is no set solution for all organizations. Later you will hear about leveraging best practices within an organization to fuel an innovation transformation (i.e., holding on). I also discuss introducing a diversity of people with new rules and tools (i.e., letting go). So, innovation really is a little bit of both holding on and letting go.

Hitting the Innovation Jackpot demystifies the blur of innovation techniques and terminology that we are all inundated with in the popular press and work every day, and drills down to what you must use to move your organization forward. However, this transformation will probably not be easy as you nudge people, organizations, and processes into uncomfortable areas along the way. This book will help you to calibrate and regulate your efforts to keep your organization executing at the highest level.

In business, it seems that most people harbor extreme feelings about innovation. To some innovation is the ultimate, while others despise it without really knowing why. In reality anything has the potential to be an innovation. Some technique or process used routinely in one domain may serve to catalyze a revolution in another domain. Therefore, even the simplest insight or approach can become an innovation when used in a new way. This book will help you to identify when, where, and how to make this transfer between different domains.

When I was coaching youth soccer, I had pairs of girls hold ropes off the ground while passing the ball back and forth as they ran down the field. This helped them to understand how to react to the ball and their teammates simultaneously. Our girls had the field spacing of a much more experienced team due to the effectiveness and fun of a drill that, to my knowledge, had never been used on a soccer field before. Since I had never coached soccer (or even played it much), I had no preconceived notions as to the "correct" drills to teach this concept. Later, I was told that soccer coaches do not normally try to teach this advanced capability at such a young age, but we found that our girls easily mastered spacing on the field with a little bit of innovation.

Hitting the Innovation Jackpot is organized as a series of essays that serve as the brick and mortar for a solid innovation framework. We attempted to make each essay a short, easily digestible message that one could read in about fifteen minutes. However, as in real life, it was impossible to make every essay the same length, so reading times range from roughly five- to forty-minutes duration. Some concepts need more time to develop, and for others, brevity of explanation actually enlivens the message.

The essays are assembled by topics tailored for individuals, teams, and organizations. Clearly teams are made up of people while organizations comprise teams, so the essays grow in dimension and build on top of one another as the book progresses. For example, the essay on the Innovation Value Chain in the "Organizations" section leverages most of the essays earlier in the book. The ultimate success of an innovation will depend on the state of the individuals, teams (i.e., groups of people), and organizational processes (i.e., policies and procedures under which teams and individuals must function). There are important ways to contribute to each layer of the innovation hierarchy, and they are provided sequentially in this book.

First, there is a methodical, systematic component that all innovation frameworks have. You need to be clear about what you will do. It is not a free-for-all but rather is pulled together by structured processes that create an approach that contains traceability, accountability, collaboration, monitoring, feedback, and measurement. Doesn't sound much like innovation, does it? However, one must remember that innovation is all about value generation, and you have to measure it before, during, and after to determine if you have actually improved your situation. This process may be subtle, or even understated, but it is always there.

Second, there is a high-touch, personal aspect of all successful innovations. This normally pertains to how a process is executed. Again, there are some timeless rules for how either a single innovation or even a company-wide innovation initiative is executed. Paramount to "how" innovation is executed is to focus on "people verbs" such as *listen* and *learn*. The most important action that any catalyst for innovation can take is to actively listen to understand , which is very much unlike the typical judgmental mode of listening that many practice. The foundation of communications supports cooperation, which in turn encourages collaboration, which eventually enables innovation. Without this sequence, great ideas will languish on supervisors' desks and superb implementation plans will go unexecuted due to lack of interest and resources.

We will examine ways to make individuals more innovative. There are some people who are more innovative than others by their very nature, and some people's personalities are diametrically opposed to all that is innovative. However, the vast majority of us are in between—not naturally innovative but trainable. People are the vital neurons of the innovation brain that you hope to assemble. With incapable and low-quality people, the potential for success is greatly reduced, so I will present ways to enhance individual, creative decision-making skills as the foundation for any innovation practice.

Once there is more than one person, you have other factors to consider such as communications, personalities, biases, and inconsistencies among team members. Teams do not naturally form in ways that enhance their probability of success. There are guidelines that can help this most action-oriented unit of an organization, the team, to perform better and more consistently. Teams will build on the communications skills of the individuals and embrace cognitive diversity to introduce a wider range of expertise into the teams. How these individuals interact with others to create effective teams will drive the next level of productivity.

The team dynamics must be considered independently from an individual's own innovative bent because innovative people who are grouped together do not necessarily form a quality innovative team. Their strengths and weaknesses may be tragically misaligned, resulting in a combination that is worse than if they had just been left to act as individuals. I will cover the critical issue of cognitive diversity and its importance to team innovation throughout this book.

An organization can have some control over the people and teams within it by providing an environment that should not only permit innovation but welcome and embrace it. This can be done by phrasing press releases in a certain way, issuing progressive policies, creating a flat organization, executing personnel reviews that reinforce innovative behavior, providing incentives tied to actions directly focused on creativity, and much more.

Organizations do not innovate—people do. However, how you form teams and establish organizations can inspire and empower individuals. Unfortunately, an organization's policies also have the potential to demoralize and marginalize individuals' efforts just as easily.

The last major premise that has stood the test of time is that there is no innovation without good execution. The greatest irony is that some of the most innovative solutions sit on the shelf until coupled with a team that has the simple capability to execute the innovation. So much emphasis is put on the act of creating but without a team of roll-up-your-sleeves implementers, you garner no value from even the greatest innovation. Organizations that herald innovation as the panacea for enduring problems force their hand on innovation, trying to do too much too quickly. I will discuss the importance of being incrementally aggressive in implementing new ideas, concepts, products, and so forth to counter this potential risk of innovation.

You will have to decide which essays fit your organization or problem best. All of these essays will not resonate with all readers. Some will excite you; some will motivate you; and some will just seem obvious to you. My objective is for you to start to form your own personal innovation attack plan for your office, your business, or your life based on these insights.

This will be the last innovation book you will ever need since it uncovers repeatable processes and timeless fundamentals that others keep recreating in case studies, each tailoring these principles to a single situation. I propose that the situation is always different. The people, the economic demands, the cultural constraints, the demographics, the state of technology, and so on all combine to create an overall environment that is different from all others. However, the basic what and how of innovation has not changed. The techniques and insights exposed in this book are provided at their most basic level to be easily applied to your unique challenge. If you internalize the principles laid out in this book at all levels of your organization, you will hit the innovation jackpot!

Individuals

Individuals with Great
Communications Skills

Communications

Most brilliant people have the ability to describe their insights and technical breakthroughs in a compelling fashion. However, truly productive people also have the commendable skill and rare inclination to see the value in listening to others in order to advance their own concepts even further.

"Great thinkers listen first."

—Michael Gelb

Listen to other people. Let the words sink in and digest them. If you are tempted to ask a question, then jot down a note so you do not forget the point that you are curious about. This intellectual restraint is a great technique that supports active listening. Take that extra step to avoid distractions that would prevent you from listening intently. In addition, writing down a question or some highlight you find useful is a sign of respect that helps to engender trust between you and the speaker.

Once the message has been absorbed, ask questions to test a hypothesis—not to impress people or belittle the speaker. A real listener does not ask a question that starts with "I was thinking …" Instead say, "You mentioned earlier … Could you comment on how you …?" The questions should be about understanding the speaker better, rather than trying to show people that you know more than the speaker.

A key roadblock to good communication is a person's tendency to evaluate. Fortunately, if you can learn to listen with understanding, you can minimize your evaluative impulses and greatly improve your communications with others (Rogers, 1991).

A major foundation in any communication is detailing the assumptions and motivations of everyone involved. These cognitive boundary conditions create a web of understanding that is often neglected. If you disagree with someone's conclusion, it is likely that you will start to argue about the conclusion. Normally, however, the reason for a disagreement is something that was *not* stated rather than something that *was* stated.

One of the key aspects of sound communication that is not given enough attention is the definition of terms. I have sat in meetings with several system engineers discussing projects and detailed engineering issues only to find out that there were several critical parameters used often in conversation during the meeting whose definitions were not agreed upon in advance.

Communications is an important factor all throughout the innovation process for both interpersonal teambuilding and derivation of a specific innovative solution. In a recent *Harvard Business Review* article David McCullough stated that, if he were asked to create a curriculum for a business school leadership program, he would focus on the criticality of listening. He would emphasize the asking of good questions and scrutinizing what people *do not* say. (McCullough, 2008)

Communication is not easy, but it must be simple! Transmitting with clarity is much more important than transmitting with volume. Below is a list of compelling communication (transmission) techniques that I have found to be useful in my career. Using the SIMPLE acronym makes them easier to remember and, therefore, to use:

	Transmission of Information (SIMPLE)
S	Stories: use stories to make a message come alive. Storytelling is a key communications technique. (Guber, 2007) Share emotion, not just facts – personalize by using "we" not "I". Be true to teller, audience, the moment, and the mission. Senses: Increase number of senses being applied, sight - even smell and touch: e.g. "Think more strategically" is not as good as "increase your intellectual stride" and "Innovation Value Chain" is better than "Innovation Process".
I	Intuition: go with your gut and what sounds right; trust your instincts.
M	Mission: focus on the mission or objective. Before each person speaks up, he or she must first restate the ideas and feelings of the previous speaker accurately and to the speaker's satisfaction.
P	Power of threes: never have more than three dimensions of a discussion. Personal: examine wants and needs – deal with wants. Use people verbs (e.g. listen, learn, etc.) and not organizational verbs (e.g. consolidate, organize, etc.); Jim Collins (management consultant and author of Built to Last and Good to Great) stated: "Do not be interesting – be interested."
L	Labels: use labels or names to get to the point and carry a message.
E	Bridging Extrema: Being counter-intuitive makes it memorable which is half of the battle (e.g. pragmatic visionary, high tech – high touch, fascinatingly mundane, etc.).

Communications can often be thought of as having three dimensions: emotional, mechanical, and cognitive (Gallo, 2010). Emotional aspects of communication are passion, inspiration, and dynamic delivery. These characteristics are difficult to teach, but it is usually easier to have the emotional dimension of communication when you are discussing a topic that is important to you. Do not just say words; tell a story. Within the first fifteen seconds of you talking, people will decide if they are going to listen to you. So do not be boring, especially at the beginning of your talk.

Cognitive dimensions of communication are easier to incorporate. Put information into intellectually manageable chunks and always speak the language of the audience.

COMMUNICATIONS

Transmit	Receive
Emotional	
Cognitive	
Mechanical	

Single presentations should take no more than fifteen to twenty minutes for optimal information transfer, largely due to the short attention span of the listeners. On a micro level, it is also important to use short words and short sentences with no extra words. Make your point and then move on.

The last component of communications, mechanics, is the easiest to change: prepare, look good, be enthusiastic, vary your pace, vary your volume, make eye contact, start strong, and finish strong.

Power is often considered someone's ability to influence people and situations around him or her. So, logically, the greater the power, the more impact one can make on a team and on individuals within that team. Yet, this sort of control actually reduces the cooperative behavior that fosters teamwork. This teamwork is needed to create new ideas. The use of power to control others not only disrupts positive interactions between team members but also emboldens the leader to actually take over the team conversations and intimidate members even more (Tost, 2011).

While an overpowering leader with a lack of tact and a large ego is clearly bad, inhibiting communication by coming to the team with a complete vision is almost as debilitating. If a team is asked to work together on a challenge that the leader has completely figured out and the leader is not willing to listen to or consider inputs from the team, this sort of environment also results in poor performance (McGoff, 2011). In all situations, it is critical for all team members—especially the leader—to communicate by both transmitting and receiving with positive intent!

"Disagree without being disagreeable."
—Ronald Reagan

While the importance of communication has always been critical, the onset of electronic media has created both opportunities and problems. E-mail, text messaging, Facebook, and Twitter are new modes of communication that can be either useful or disastrous! E-mails seem almost archaic to many people in their day-to-day lives, but it is still the workhorse of business communications, as it provides the ability to communicate a complex message to whomever you want to receive it.

Some classic techniques to manage the crush of e-mails and maximize their utility are basic skills that people can also use in face-to-face communications:

- Give your reader the complete context at the start of your message. Do not make them read all of the previous threads of the message to be able to respond.
- Write e-mails with a sensitivity to the fact that people are busy. Get to the point!
- Use a subject line to summarize and convince the recipient to read your e-mail.
- When you copy more than three people (a practice that should be used sparingly), explain why each person should care. Do not waste peoples' time. Time is the most valuable resource for your colleagues and for you.
- Use blind carbon copy (bcc) only when the identities of recipients need to be protected. Always tell the recipients of the use of the bcc.
- The only reason you should be sending a message to many people is to give them a document or to coordinate information such as a meeting time. Never try to have a conversation or dialogue with more than three people! *The probability that you will receive a response to an e-mail is inversely proportional to the number of recipients.*
- Make action requests clear. It is best to put in the title of the e-mail "ACTION REQUIRED" or "ACTION REQUESTED" to make sure that there is no confusion.
- Never type an e-mail when you are angry.
- Assume that anything that you put in an e-mail will end up in the most embarrassing location (such as your boss's e-mail, the local newspaper, or your spouse's desk).

Unfortunately, in this day and age, communication norms cannot be discussed without considering texting, Facebook, and Twitter. The real success metric in any online network is that it solves social problems that cannot be solved offline, for example, through quick connections across long distances and across social demographics. Texting and tweeting are very simple and use limited words, so information is usually passed without proper context. This can be a problem since short messages received without an understanding of the sender's motive or situation can be easily misinterpreted. Facebook, on the other hand, is the other extreme. There is often almost too much context *and* content. Unfortunately, more information can sometimes be used for evil than for good if you have not vetted both the current *and* future intentions of your so-called friends.

The most interesting insight about Facebook is that it is primarily about pictures: 70 percent of all actions are related to viewing pictures or viewing other people's profiles. The most frequent visual users are men looking at women they don't know, followed by men looking at women they do know. This is a little embarrassing for the male gender, as two-thirds of all page views are of women's pages by men. In this way, online networks can be used as cover for less than forthright activities (e.g., job hunting, social spying, gossiping, etc.). Many users create relationships with others to stay in touch with peers and to make new contacts. Social media allows them to establish plausible deniability that they are not looking for jobs, even if they are (Silverthorne, 2009).

Twitter is different; women proportionately use it more than men. MySpace is seen as being passé and is not used very much, yet as of 2011, MySpace actually had seventy million US users, while Facebook had around one hundred million users. Twitter only had twenty million users in the United States. MySpace focuses on users in places where they don't have much contact with people who create news that gets read by others. In addition, the MySpace user generally makes less money than the average Facebook user. At the time of the writing of this book, statistics showed that Facebook user growth was slowing; a mathematical inevitability due to its initial explosive growth (Silverthorne, 2009).

> **"It's better to keep your mouth shut and appear to be stupid than to open it and remove all doubt."**
>
> —Abraham Lincoln

I recently attended a local gathering of Chief Technology Officers at which the guest speaker discussed social media and Enterprise 2.0. The speaker, Dion Hinchcliffe of Dachis Group, provided a statistic showing that social networking passed e-mail as having the most interactions between people in 2007 and continues to grow faster. I contend that more data and more connections are not necessarily better; rather, better data and better connections are what we need. Unfortunately, "better" is very difficult to measure.

So in that light, I hypothesize that Facebook and other social media are great to maintain and enrich existing friendships that have been formulated through old-fashioned face-to-face chats, shopping outings, or poker games, but it is not a great place to start a friendship. The two are not equal. Dion hinted at this concept as he quoted Clay Shirky, who said, "Information overload is not the problem. It's filter failure." I believe that the filter needs to be some foundation of real personal interaction that occurs *before* using the power of social networking; social networking should not be allowed to *replace* personal interactions. I will discuss this more in the essay "High Tech, High Touch."

Listen, Learn, and Write Things Down

Years ago I became frustrated when I repeatedly encountered situations that I knew had been introduced to me previously in books, conversations, or even past failures or successes. Yet, I just could not harvest the information from my feeble memory for my own use when I needed it. These books were already published or the events long since passed. I just wanted the two to three relevant sentences that I could retrieve and apply to my specific situation.

Of course, none of us have perfect memories, so how can we increase our chances of applying relevant information in the future?

I started to write down tidbits of useful information from these publications and encounters and stuff them into my briefcase. Soon, I was getting buried in little shards of knowledge. About ten years ago, I realized that I was collecting information in four major areas: technology, innovation, people, and strategy. These topics created a convenient acronym, TIPS. I started to type up these morsels of insight into a simple Word document.

I have maintained and grown this asset over the years. I make a habit of reading the now 125-page document at least once a quarter. Each time I have examined this treasure trove of quotes, excerpts, insights, ideas, and so forth I find something that is useful for my current endeavors. I really mean *always*. I have everything from article excerpts to comments made by professional colleagues at formal meetings to personal musings I committed to paper after watching a special on TV.

After relating the utility of the TIPS document to colleagues, I found that many, maybe even most, colleagues were intimidated by the prospect of reading over one hundred pages of content-rich, disjointed facts and insights. As a result, I started to prepare monthly book reports that provided summaries of books, articles, and papers that I had read the previous month. (By the way, in addition to old-fashioned books, I have found the Harvard Business School's "Working Knowledge" newsletter as well as *Fast Company* magazine to be the two best consistently useful periodicals for my techno-innovative-cognitive bent.)

My new book report product is a hybrid of Executive Book Summaries and a multidisciplinary blog with a thread of innovation philosophy running through it all. The book reports are much smaller and less imposing than my TIPS document, so they are almost always read by others, unlike the bulky TIPS collection.

The positive comments and dialogue created by the sharing of these bite-sized pieces of insight provided me with the impetus to write *Hitting the Innovation Jackpot*. People are just so busy now, but being introduced to multiple, seemingly disparate domains so critical to innovative thought, I knew I had to provide a treatise on innovation that could be *the* unifying framework. Unlike my massive TIPS document, this book is the coherent, refined compilation of my thoughts as I have reflected upon all of these documents and my own personal experiences in responding to real-world challenges over thirty years.

A key aspect of my process has been the open sharing of this information with anyone who is interested. The resulting dialogue with people has been the genesis and catalyst for many of the most useful insights in this book.

On a similar note, an interesting tradition that Israeli travelers and tourists started in places all over the world is a log of useful facts, warnings, and hints related to a specific locale (e.g., a hotel or park). This tradition is now followed by many people, but it is still clearly an Israeli invention (Senor, 2009). The book is an exemplar for listening, learning, and writing things down to benefit others.

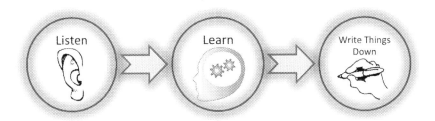

As I was completing this manuscript, I bought the book *3-Minute Einstein* by Paul Parsons. He broke down the scientific and historical legacy of Einstein into three-minute chunks. The book is fabulous and did for the life and work of Einstein what I hope to do for innovation with this book. My goal is to make a huge amount of work on a complex topic available to the public in a form that is easy to digest, understand, and use. Parsons has made Einstein accessible to many more people through this practical approach.

However, sometimes writing something down is not necessarily composing eloquent text but, rather, merely drawing a picture. As a matter of fact, Einstein developed most of his great theories by drawing pictures first. As his career progressed, he had to do more with math, and it has been speculated that this focus on analytics over drawing resulted in fewer great breakthroughs later in Einstein's career (Parsons, 2011).

Many scientists use inductive reasoning by trawling through experimental data, trying to spot trends and draw inferences from them. However, starting to solve a problem by simplifying it first into a single image provides three critical aspects of innovation: acting, sharing, and building.

First, the act of drawing or even doodling as the initial part of a brainstorming process provides the simple act of initiation. So many great solutions have never materialized because would-be inventors never started. Drawing is often simpler for people than writing. Anyone can draw a box and a few lines plus an arrow or two.

Second, drawing a picture provides a way to share your thoughts with other people quickly and explicitly. You can pass around a picture, debate about the size and direction of boxes and the placement of arrows and captions. Many, if not most, people are visual thinkers, so you are likely to get people to contribute to an evolving concept much more easily with a diagram.

This leads to the third step, building. As the figure grows in size and complexity, the solution is being built one step at a time. Converting the essence of the picture to text enables the maturing of the concept into a complete solution. Members of the team can then review detailed explanations of individual components, with the framework of the picture binding them together.

The panel below shows two figures that I helped to develop as part of a National Research Council (NRC) committee on assessing NASA's Micrometeoroid and Orbital Debris (MMOD) program in 2011. I found that the members of the highly talented and diverse group were talking past each other on key issues of technical and operational significance. I proposed the upper figure (A) as a starting point for discussions. I did not put everything that I knew about the topic into the figure in order to facilitate content-rich, focused discussions without too much of my own bias.

After several hours of very productive face-to-face dialogue with this ten-person team, the figure had evolved into *our* understanding. It was not Darren's figure anymore. This framework was then added to and modified by every member over the last few months of that effort. Figure B (lower figure) was the final form of the depiction that was used as a unifying construct in the report that was delivered to NASA and others.

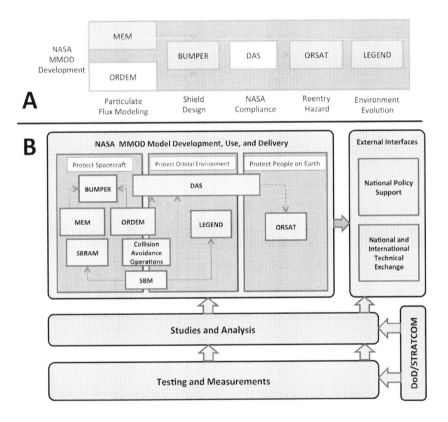

This figure went through ten distinct revisions that captured well over a hundred specific individual contributions. This laborious exercise in "listen, learn, and write things down" not only contributed mightily to the final study *product*, but it also streamlined the *process* of completing this complex assessment (National Research Council, 2011).

While listening is fairly simple to encourage and monitor, learning is more complex and more interactive, as learning often requires public debate. The fear of being wrong can be crippling to many people, so it often restrains peoples' debating behavior. A useful technique in this process is to not assert truths but rather pose alternative hypotheses. Analysis will support or refute hypotheses. It should not condemn you as being wrong. Personalize discussions, but depersonalize analysis, to ensure that people do not hold back. You must allow people to propose new ideas without the fear of being wrong. The biggest breakthroughs often occur when someone is brave enough to say, "I do not understand," or to say something that sounds incredibly stupid (at first).

The evolution of the figures in the NRC report was a good example of how I took one step back to help us take two steps forward. I did not worry about appearing to be confused. In addition, it is a great example of when the process is more important than the product. The figure itself did not provide any vital insights, but the process of creating it catalyzed discussions between team members that enabled exchange and assimilation of information that would not have happened otherwise. This increased information exchange improved the overall quality of the report more than the figure itself.

"The team that makes the most mistakes will probably win."

—Piggy Lambert, John Wooden's basketball coach

Do not be the person with all of the answers; rather, be the one with the thoughtful questions that help others to get to the right answers on their own (or with you). Remember the old adage, "There are no dumb questions"? Well, clearly that is wrong. There are many dumb, useless, counterproductive questions. However, thoughtful questions posed to illuminate and clarify rather than intimidate, embarrass, or impress can be incredibly valuable. The process of enquiry is often more important than the product (i.e., the answer).

Ask questions that provide people with the option of no losers when responding to it. When doubting the utility of an approach or questioning someone else's concepts, carefully consider how you phrase your questions. Avoid poor poorly worded questions such as, "I have found that your approach has always failed in the past. Why do you think it will be any different this time? I have suffered through previous failures and don't look forward to making the same mistake again." Use good phrasing when asking questions, for example, "I am not sure that I have seen the approach you have suggested before. What are the primary benefits and limitations of this approach from your experience?"

Quality people often underperform because they are afraid of showing any weakness by asking a question. For high achievers, looking stupid or incompetent is not acceptable. They would rather do the wrong thing well than the right thing poorly (DeLong, 2011).

In contrast, I often refer to my role in some meetings as "wearing the pointy hat" (i.e., a dunce's cap). This does not mean that I act stupid (on purpose). However, I also do *not* have as a metric that people walk away thinking that I am smart. I have sat in meetings for hours trying to help people solve difficult problems about complex pieces of hardware and advanced software applications where very smart people seemed to not be listening to each other.

While I often am accused of taking a step backward (as I did on the NRC deliberations), I will often ask people to express some fundamental observation for that venue such as how system engineering principles might be useful in solving the problem. I might state that I was not sure who in the room had responsibility for each major component: requirements definition, design documentation, testing, and so on. As you might imagine, my "silly questions" often allow people a chance to agree on terminology and identify their respective roles in the solution process. I will discuss more on this dynamic later in the essay "Innovation Value Chain."

"Einstein made many mistakes but he was not afraid of making mistakes."

—Paul Parsons

Even as a leader, it is okay to do some stumbling and bumbling. When I was a physics professor at the US Air Force Academy, the student population was uniquely talented and confident, so when they succumbed to their first college physics course I was there to pick up the pieces. As a matter of fact, I am not even a physicist, yet I taught electricity and magnetism, a freshman-level core physics course. I made a conscious effort to return to the physics classroom as a practicing aerospace engineer to provide a level of pragmatism that I felt had been lacking when I took physics.

Physics class is often depicted with the stereotypical eccentric professor scribbling some derivations wildly on the chalkboard, with his back to the classroom, periodically grunting approval of the fine job he is doing. In my experience, the typical physics professor almost seemed to relish the confused, dazed looks of the students that he caught out of the corner of his eye. *Confusion* was followed by *dismay*, which was quickly accompanied by his friend, *despair*. It was this despair that you were often left to take back to your dorm room with you and share the next two days with until you had a chance of making sense of that foreign language at the next class meeting.

Actually, without a little bit of confusion, it is likely that members of the team (i.e., the office or class) are not progressing individually or collectively. This dynamic tension is captured by what I told my cadets in my classroom: "You learn the most just after a slight period of confusion."

This is true in the classroom, in the boardroom, on the athletic field, and all over. However, burying someone in facts and jargon before proceeding headlong into dismay and despair misses the opportunity presented by confusion. Confusion is the brain creating new connections; it is equivalent to intense exercise creating muscle mass. However, if you go too far, the muscle and the brain do not come out better than before. They are just left damaged, and no progress is made.

In my assertion that you learn the most just after a slight period of confusion, "just after" means that the leader must pause and have the team members truly reflect on how to arrange this new cacophony of information into an intelligible axiom or fact. Here, silence is our friend. Stop talking and let the jumbled shapes and sizes of facts fall into a more organized arrangement in your mind or your teammates' minds. Just like shaking a bag of trail mix and staring down until you can better see if any M&Ms are left, you must pause and actually think.

The figure below depicts three points along the spectrum of information processing and confusion, with the middle ostensibly being the optimum. However, only you can determine the proper mix for your team, for the given time, place, and problem set. Clearly, the key is the balance between transmitting and receiving among individuals on a team, in a classroom, in a lab, on the field, and so on.

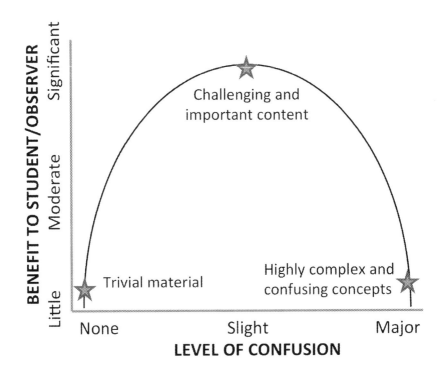

Often in sports, people will say, "No pain, no gain." Just as there was a difference between confusion and despair in my physics classroom, there is a difference between discomfort and pain in sports. As a longtime coach of youth sports and a sports competitor myself, the difference between discomfort and pain is mostly its duration. Anything that lingers well past the initial event is pain; discomfort fades quickly when someone is being properly trained. So intellectually it is critical that you are confused often about problems and answers; just do not let this confusion linger into despair. Despair will not empower innovation but a little confusion can.

Even when I was a student at the Air Force Academy, I had already started applying my favorite saying, "Listen, learn, and write things down." However, in retrospect, I can see that it very well could have been "Listen, write things down so you can learn." I was well known for my near-microfiche index cards on which I would cram all of the salient facts for an upcoming test of such simple courses as Thermodynamics or Law for Military Officers. I did this so I would have the material at the ready to study when I had a few spare minutes in study hall or standing in formation (remember, this was a military academy). I even used to pull them out before the lights went down at the movie theater while on dates. Sadly, this is not an exaggeration, as my wife of thirty years can attest. What I discovered from writing these study cards was that the process of organizing and writing down the material really helped me to learn the material so much better. As a result, it is always *listen* first, but you pick what comes second and third.

Listening, learning, and writing things down are three simple acts that combine to create a unique value proposition, and the concept hints at a key theme of this book: people verbs are the key to enabling innovation.

"If it is not written down, then it does not exist."

—Darren McKnight

Innovation Exemplar: Crossword Puzzle

Crossword puzzles exercise many cognitive aspects of innovation: memory, inference, deduction, and creativity. The ability to extract explicit knowledge (i.e., exercise your memory) from many domains is critical to generating new ideas. Knowledge of simple information does not define innovation; however, individual facts do serve as building blocks for innovation.

Below are several sets of crossword puzzle clues that I created, highlighting the different cognitive challenges these puzzles usually provide. Cover up the right column and see if you can figure these out on your own:

North of Oregon	washington
Marching band composer	sousa
Vice president	biden
Killer bacteria	anthrax
Santa Ana _____	winds
Solid furniture wood	oak

Other clues require simple association rather than the extraction of explicit knowledge. Some examples are shown below in columns so you can test yourself. Simple association is a combination of explicit knowledge and the ability to extrapolate slightly. Solving these often requires a little bit of help from other words in the crossword to limit the options since there may be multiple possible answers.

Home of the brave?	usa
Type of eng.	mech
Perry of song?	como
Digit ready to shoot	itchy
Nasty dispenser of cola?	jerk
Crazy clock?	cuckoo

The most difficult clues require complex associations. These are a combination of explicit knowledge, creative interpretation, and the ability to examine the question from alternative perspectives. There is normally at least a two-step process for complex associations. First, you need to determine what context or domain is relevant and then determine the answer within that domain.

One common quandary is figuring out if the word is a noun or verb. The following words can have widely different solutions depending on if each is intended as a noun or as a verb: race, leave, text, storm. The fixation on answers for *race* as a noun will make it very difficult to come up with *speed* as the reasonable answer for *race* as a verb.

Other complex associations may be nothing more than cute plays on words that cannot be solved until some of the correct words have been put in place on the puzzle. If you get none of these correct below, do not worry; these almost always have multiple right answers and can only be solved in a crossword puzzle with some of the other words already filled in first.

Web concern	connection or link (for the internet)
	silk or bug (for spider)
Knife	utensil (as a cutter)
	dart (as a verb)

19

Between a and b	bflat (for music)
Al Capone	scarface (for nickname)
	gangster (for role)
Clean surfers?	bleachboys (play on words)
Jack follower	jill (for nursery rhyme)
	knife (for swim/dive)
	lyndon (for president)

Doing crossword puzzles helps people to practice thinking from different perspectives; inferring or guessing from limited knowledge; and reinforcing explicit knowledge. If you have done crossword puzzles before, you also know that they amplify the pitfall of having a wrong answer early. This is also true for innovation, as when a team gets pulled in a certain direction due to the psychological inertia of the group, it is very difficult to identify and modify any preliminary falsehoods.

One of the most intriguing aspects of doing a crossword puzzle, as with tackling any challenging problem, is your plan of attack. There are three typical ways in which I solve crossword puzzles, and each its own pros and cons that parallel real-world problem solving:

- *I Have a Plan*: Start with the first across clue and methodically try all of the across clues first. Be careful to lightly fill in clues in which you have only slight confidence. Next, do the down clues in reverse order and work your way back up the puzzle. This requires discipline and being a good judge of clues you may or may not know. This is similar to executing on a real project. It is very difficult to recover from an incorrect clue filled in early, just as if your project rules out the use of a specific method that later may have been found to be very useful.
- *Easy Does It*: Fill-in-the-blank clues are considered the easiest, so do all of those first. Shorter words are typically easier than longer words, so try those words next. From the words you have

filled in, try the clues next to where you have filled in the first letter of the answer. After this initial solution process, fill in the clues with the fewest letters left. This is a great approach for a project-completion strategy, if you have the luxury of doing all of the easiest tasks first, especially when their completion actually contributes to solving the more difficult challenges.

- *Take What I Can Get*: In this final approach, you start as if you are using the "I Have a Plan" approach, but once you get a word filled in, you attempt to fill in words that are connected to that answer. Continue to work out from this starting point, but when you lose momentum, go back to the "I Have A Plan" tactic. This hybrid approach is often the optimal one as you leverage your existing clues the best, just like, in real-life, being able to address a problem in a variety of ways is often the most effective and efficient method.

I must warn you that some studies have concluded that doing crossword puzzles does not help individuals to enhance their overall cognitive proficiency. These studies say that, at best, it merely makes you better at doing crossword puzzles. I think that it depends on how you do them, just like anything else in life.

If you do crossword puzzles and relish the interesting cognitive biases your brain grapples with in completing puzzles, then you can benefit more deeply. For instance, when you read the clue "ride in space" and immediately think of "soar," "rocket," and "float," and then see that "sally" is the answer, you'll think about how you will not be led astray the next time and you will hone your analytical skills. Every time I get tricked or almost get tricked, I remind myself to be open-minded and creative in how I approach all written and spoken material. This intellectual sharpness will help you in all walks of your life.

INNOVATION – Cognitive Jumping Jacks

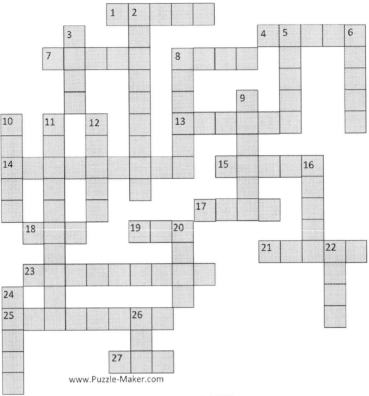

www.Puzzle-Maker.com

ACROSS
1 time's partner
4 try to avoid tag
7 main artery
8 café au ___
13 power of _____
14 right before you learn the most
15 great thinkers listen _____
17 telescopic disc
18 nuke
19 quirky
21 short treatise
23 card game at the hook and ladder
25 famous physicist/artist?
27 CIA forerunner

DOWN
2 practical
3 song by John Denver, Perhaps _____
5 takes treasure from
8 most critical verb of communications
9 surrogate for innovation
10 Yale produces them
11 systematic creativity
12 Halloween decoration
16 groups of individuals
20 profound
22 call to feed the kitty
24 "Maybelline" singer
26 hospital hookups

Answers to the crossword puzzle are at the end of the book.

In What Quadrant Do You Live?

Good ideas, new insights, and unique solutions do not grow if you have to continually react to tasks assigned to you by others. This reactionary environment gives you no time to think and do things for yourself. While everyone cannot be the leader of his or her organization or team, you must be the leader of how you lead your life. I propose that there are three worlds in which we can live:

- Placate: We react to others' demands simply to survive.
- Anticipate: We plan and prepare to enable our own success.
- Rejuvenate: We act to replenish our energy and capabilities.

I provide the chart below to my clients in order to remind them to not get stuck in the tactical (placate) quadrant. I suggest that they put this diagram on their bulletin boards to remind them of the importance of their office style on their ability to innovate.

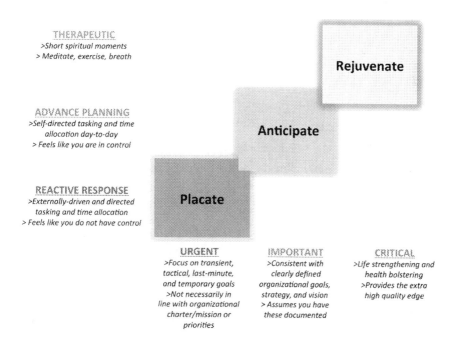

THERAPEUTIC
>Short spiritual moments
> Meditate, exercise, breath

Rejuvenate

ADVANCE PLANNING
>Self-directed tasking and time
allocation day-to-day
> Feels like you are in control

Anticipate

REACTIVE RESPONSE
>Externally-driven and directed
tasking and time allocation
> Feels like you do not have control

Placate

URGENT
>Focus on transient,
tactical, last-minute,
and temporary goals
>Not necessarily in
line with organizational
charter/mission or
priorities

IMPORTANT
>Consistent with
clearly defined
organizational goals,
strategy, and vision
> Assumes you have
these documented

CRITICAL
>Life strengthening and
health bolstering
>Provides the extra
high quality edge

23

In what quadrant do you spend most of your time?

It is critical that you balance your activities daily, weekly, monthly, and annually so that you plan and prepare for important tasks. Do not let the world pull you into reacting to their urgent demands, or else you will not have any control where you end up. Even when you are the most junior person in an office, you do not have to be beholden to what others tell you to do, how to do it, and when to do it. Take charge and get your work requirements documented and then create a plan to execute on your own timetable. More importantly, it is critical to do things that not only satisfy other demands immediately but also lay the foundation for independent thought and performance through core-building activities. These rejuvenating efforts include meditating, doing crossword puzzles, exercising, deep breathing, and more.

Ron Alexander explained in an interview how he grew a business of therapy and executive coaching for creative workers such as Hollywood producers, musicians, screenwriters, and the advertising elite. He stated that meditating for only twelve minutes daily provided a "mind strength" that contributed to better problem-solving abilities. This approach worked for any profession since it was based on being more attuned to what you were doing and the people around you (Kamenetz, 2011). Clearly, he is endorsing regular efforts to rejuvenate, as discussed above.

This can work for a professional of any age since the brain is actually still capable of improving no matter how old you are. Joshua Aronson, a psychologist from New York University, has even shown that people can continue to make brain cells (called neurogenesis) throughout their lives. More brain cells provide more pathways to solve problems and recall information. The more you challenge yourself, the better you perform. I consider exercise, both physical and intellectual, to be an "anticipate" activity, bordering on rejuvenation. However, at the same time, someone who spends all of their time rejuvenating brings no one any value!

The key is balancing these three quadrants. I suggest that the best combination, though difficult to achieve, is with the vast majority of time going into anticipating, with smaller amounts of placating and rejuvenating in equal measure. However, most of the people that I know spend more than

80 percent of their time placating, allocating little time to either anticipating or rejuvenating.

The connection between intelligence and creativity has not been characterized well. However, analogs of executive functions such as planning, integrating, and abstract thinking can be improved by mindful meditation such as introspective thinking and physiological support (e.g., deep breathing). Meditation can not only improve intelligence (showing gains in IQ points) but can also aid in logical thinking by cleaning the conscious brain of trivial facts and details that will then permit more relevant information to be recognized. This is similar to the "nonmindful" meditation of just taking your mind off a mental challenge for a while and finding that when you come back to it, the right answer to a perplexing problem jumps right out at you (Kamenetz, 2011).

I find this a lot when I do something as simple as a crossword puzzle or as complex as solving an analysis dilemma. I will be struggling with a certain region of the puzzle in which several words just seem impossible to find, but if I drop the puzzle for about an hour or so and then come back, I often find one of those seemingly impossible words almost immediately. I let the previous context and preconceptions that were making the solution hard to find (i.e., psychological inertia) disappear, and coming back afresh is often all that is needed. In other words, while it is seemingly counterintuitive, sometimes you need to slow down to solve problems more quickly.

I talk often about "Starbucks time." This is not about the coffee as much as it is about slowing down and picking the order and pace with which you address problems. Never use the Wi-Fi at Starbucks. That defeats the purpose of unplugging yourself from the speed of electronic transactions and replacing it with the firing of your neurons. Move yourself out of the placate zone and into anticipating, or even beyond to rejuvenating.

Even when you are in the office, do not check e-mails all day. Pick three regular times (e.g., 8 a.m., 11 a.m., and 3 p.m.) each day to check e-mails. Do not let that incessant beeping prioritize your entire day every day! Do not let Outlook be yet another taskmaster!

"Failing to prepare is preparing to fail."

—John Wooden

While it is often possible for you to control how you respond to your work and home environment by living in the right quadrant, can this affect how an entire nation's culture has evolved? The establishment of a robust technology-based economy in Israel was driven by certain attributes of the Jewish state and culture that produced highly innovative and effective teams that could be, at least partially, applied to other situations.

Israel has many more start-ups per capita than any other country in the world. This is important for a country's overall economy, as US statistics have shown that most of the net employment gains between 1980 and 2005 came from firms less than five years old. Israel is a small country surrounded by enemies, a situation that provides a feeling of isolation that does not seem to be conducive to entrepreneurial innovation. Yet, that dire situation has driven the Israeli culture and economy. Several purposeful and accidental features of how Israelis act provide indicators for the innovation engine that has developed there over the last thirty years. The Israelis have risen above the adversity and isolation with tenacity (i.e., chutzpah) (Senor, 2009).

This combination of geographic and cultural hardships has strengthened and honed Israelis' capability to be creative with limited resources. While we need not be threatened as a nation or group and encircled by enemies to become innovative, this can be a catalyst for breakthroughs. Israel had to work hard to anticipate threats, and falling into a "placate" state would have likely proven catastrophic.

High Tech, High Touch

"High tech, high touch" is an evolving theme of the third millennium, with contrasts between extremes being all important. In 1982, John Naisbitt's book *Megatrends* first identified the importance of "high touch" in response to new technology, yet that dichotomy is getting more pronounced and important every year. One-dimensional technical experts or one-dimensional touchy-feely types will not be successful. An amalgamation of techniques, approaches, and concepts across the entire spectrum will be required to excel.

The quote below by Margaret Wheatley provides emotional inspiration that can propel highly technical projects to success. The passion that exudes from this excerpt is what must be coupled with sound technical tools to power innovation in the future.

> **"Thinking is the place where intelligent actions begin. There is no distance between thinking and acting when the ideas mean something to us. When we look thoughtfully at a situation and understand its destructive dynamics, we act to change it. Governments and organizations struggle with implementation since inside any bureaucracy there's a huge gap between ideas and actions. But this is because we don't care about those ideas. We will not take risks for something we do not believe in. But when it's your idea, a result of thinking, and we see how it might truly benefit our lives, then we act immediately on any promising notion."**
>
> —Margaret Wheatley

High tech, high touch; sweet and sour; thunder and lightning; and rock and roll are all timeless pairs that live on well past their creation to produce excitement. You must have excitement to have success! The magic of two extremes blending into one powerful spirit is alive and well in most innovation. In the first essay of this book, I identified bridging the extrema in the Communications essay as a valuable technique to enable a more memorable and remember-able title (e.g., pragmatic visionary).

All successful innovation is a mixture of high tech and high touch. While many treatises on innovation pick one mode or the other, it is clear that true value-generating, reproducible, and long-lasting innovations come from a mixture of high-tech and high-touch techniques.

You must live your world in both camps and constantly change the emphasis back and forth while raising your entire level of competence. If you do all of one or the other, the foundation will be weak and will collapse. If, on your way toward success, you weave back and forth between high tech and high touch, then you are stronger at the end.

While the hypothesis of this essay is that this balance has always been the true discriminator in innovation, the 2006 Council on Competitiveness, sponsored by the US Congress, pointedly suggested that a variety of economic and demographic realities make success in the twenty-first century more based on "complex communication and creative thinking skills over manual and routine cognitive skills."

People *do* innovation; it does not just happen. People *do* innovation by acting, not just by thinking "great thoughts." However, high-touch activities may not seem very innovative:

- *Listen*: This does not sound very active or insightful, but it is the crux of the beginning of all innovation.
- *Learn*: This occurs only after one listens to new material and understands it in one's own perspective.
- *Leverage*: This is a loaded word that emphasizes the cross-domain application of existing techniques to bring value.

As a complement to the three *L*'s of high-touch innovation, the three *A*'s of high-tech innovation are:

- *Awareness*: This is the perception of new knowledge or techniques. This is relative to the observer and is critical to performing activities more efficiently.
- *Analysis:* While analysis is important, you must be careful not to overanalyze. Systematic processes must be used to provide organization and traceability; however, tracking too many metrics, variables, and so on may create what is referred to as "paralysis by analysis."
- *Action:* Technology enables and accelerates action. The use of collaboration tools, enterprise applications, business intelligence utilities, and more can empower innovation when coupled with high-touch axioms.

While I emphasized the importance of communicating smartly when listening, talking, and writing, actions are an important extension of those techniques. Behavior is another important form of communication. It not only can reinforce words, but it also provides an example for others to follow. Some say that a picture is worth a thousand words; well, then behavior is worth a thousand pictures. Dr. Nido Qubein, HPU President, goes one layer deeper in his foreword to this book by extolling how beliefs drive behaviors. Therefore, while action is important, it will be largely based on the beliefs that you embrace.

"The best thing a man can do for his children is to love their mother."

—Abraham Lincoln

Blending art and science; high tech and high touch; and rules and tools all are key innovation themes. I believe that mankind has neither continued to evolve through linear stages nor held social constituents constant. Conversely, society has oscillated between two extremes. Mankind has weathered the complex introduction, developing, maturation, and dying off of multiple diverse trends that have aggregated to create a cyclical function between an emphasis on technology and an emphasis on people skills: high tech versus high touch. The figure below portrays this general oscillating sequence over the millennia. This figure is not drawn to scale and is merely intended to highlight the fact that the relationships between humans and their societies do not stay constant over time.

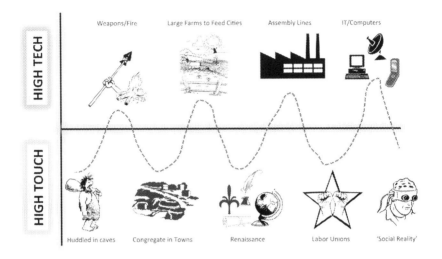

I propose that the current momentum toward computing and information technology will oscillate back toward a social reality in which social media is extended to include more personal interactions that will counter much of the current context-less content that is now propagated on social media sites. Emotion and passion are difficult to portray in pure text, though people seem to understand the difference between ☺ and #$@&*^$%. Social reality will advance the truly personal aspects of interactions through holographic technologies, the capture of individual emissions (e.g., heat, movement, etc.) that reflect emotive state, virtual body language, and more.

The pace of information exchange cannot continue to increase without some modulation providing the uniquely human instinct that can never be captured on a computer chip. This will help to fuel the next generation of creativity that will be enabled by technology. As my musical mentor likes to say, "Content drives technology!"

"I've learned that people will forget what you said, people will forget what you did, but people will never forget how you made them feel."

—Maya Angelou

Creativity is the process of generating new ideas; this process is enabled by divergent thinking and cognitive flexibility. Divergent thinking is the ability to create new ideas and consider varied solutions to a single problem by learning to ignore limits that others may consider sacrosanct. Conversely, cognitive flexibility is the skill of rearranging information as a function of a given situation in order to maximize one's own personal utility (Gino, 2011).

Creativity has been critical for both human progress and adaptation. This has made it a common topic for scholars to study and understand its sources and how to increase it. Because creativity improves problem solving and opens doors to new solutions, many assume that creativity should be encouraged. However, can we be sure that more creativity is always better? Gino initiated research to determine if there might be some negative aspects of creativity. Any of you who are parents know the answer: absolutely!

Clearly, a child who is very cognitively flexible and capable of widely divergent thinking will be a challenge. I will digress for a moment and assert that, at least from a parenting perspective, if anchored with strong morals, a child who is able to be very creative always turns out better in the long run than those children who never test the boundaries.

Gino, however, examined specifically the relationship between dishonesty and creativity in adults. He found that people who were encouraged to think beyond their comfort zones often used unethical workarounds to address challenges. He showed that there was indeed a positive correlation between creativity and cheating or dishonesty. Taken to the extreme, many criminals have this ability to envision a drastically different set of operating conditions than what normal law-abiding society will accept, which leads them to their nonconformist actions. Therefore, there might actually be a limit to how much creativity is positive.

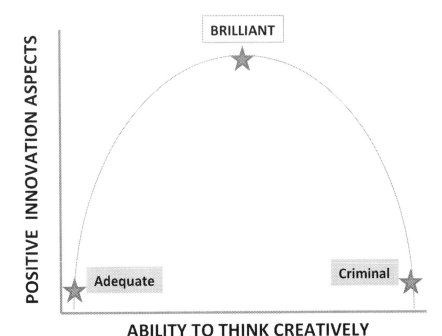

I would like to reiterate Dr. Qubein's statement in the foreword: "Creativity is about doing things differently. Innovation is about doing things better." The implication is clear but important to repeat. Innovation is doing something new that brings value, not just doing something new. Positive passion and personal intent (i.e., high touch) must continue to be emphasized even as technology breakthroughs occur at a seemingly ever-accelerating pace.

> **"We are in the twilight of a society based on data. As information and intelligence become the domain of computers, society will place a new value on the one human ability that can't be automated: Emotion."**
>
> —Craig Anderton

Healthy Body = Creative Mind

Physical fitness and cognitive fitness are intimately related. They are intertwined, as being in better physical shape helps the functioning of your brain, which in turn enhances your cognitive abilities. Similarly, if you work hard to listen and learn while applying what you've learned to create better solutions, you will be more likely to assimilate the facts that reflect the importance of being physically fit. Even if the result of a healthy lifestyle were only living longer to be able to innovate more, it would be beneficial. However, it also improves your ability to function cognitively by providing the most efficient brain possible during your entire lifetime. Until now, studies have shown that exercise helps lower blood pressure, bad cholesterol, insulin levels, and all risk factors for strokes (Neurology, 2011).

Research showed that the following activities contributed the most to preventing dementia (most important first):

- aerobic exercise
- education
- genetics
- deliberate practice
- complex professions
- communication skills
- optimism
- unselfishness
- number of leisure activities
- types of food (antioxidants and anti-inflammatories)
- reduction of caloric intake

Complex physical activity is even more beneficial than simple aerobic exercise. Recent research reinforced this fact, as brain cells in rats given acrobatic training were found to have a greater number of synapses per cell than inactive rats or rats given only physical exercise. Studies showed that exercising for one hour, three times a week, for three months produced increased cerebral flow; enhanced memory; lowered blood pressure;

and increased neurogenesis (the making of new baby neurons that link disparate information) (Strauch, 2010). My personal experience supports this assertion, as I feel lethargic and dull-witted when I get out of my normal workout routine.

Exercise produces new brain cells in a fairly straightforward way. When muscles contract they produce growth factors. Normally, those growth-factor molecules are too large to make it through the blood-brain barrier, but for reasons that are still unknown, exercise makes that barrier more porous, allowing those growth factors, once referred to as "Miracle-Gro for the brain," to get through and help stimulate neuron growth (Strauch, 2010).

Recent studies have shown that even elderly people (older than seventy years old) who regularly exercise at moderate to intense levels may have a 40 percent lower risk of developing certain kinds of dementia and mobility problems. Research published in the journal *Neurology* presented studies showing that subjects who exercised at higher levels were significantly less likely to show brain damage caused by blocked arteries that interrupt blood flow, which could trigger strokes, than people who exercised lightly. There was no difference between those who exercised lightly and those who did not exercise at all. Exercise has emerged as the great equalizer for brain fitness. Physical exercise of just walking thirty minutes about five days a week improves mental health (Habits, 2010). As I stated earlier you must challenge yourself to improve. Discomfort, but not necessarily pain, *is* a reasonable objective.

Evidence suggests mental exercise can contribute to keeping the brain functioning optimally, but we must stay engaged and challenged with intellectually diverse activities. The dentate gyrus is where new brain cells (actually stem cells) are primarily produced. New neurons are produced when we focus on tasks that are highly complex, but we also know that only half of new brain cells survive. So you are always fighting an uphill physical and cognitive battle, especially after the age of thirty. As a result, one really needs to be making a lot of new brain cells to have a significant net growth because some of the old, existing ones are also dying off. Rats living in challenging and stimulating environments had dendrites in their cerebral cortex that had longer branches when compared to rats housed in isolated conditions. Crossword puzzles also provide a simple means to continually keep learning through deliberate, challenging cognitive work.

As discussed earlier, completing crossword puzzles are not just any kind of cognitive exercise. It is the best since it works many modes of thinking just like an exercise that engages many muscle groups simultaneously is particularly versatile. Sudoku or word scramblers work only one aspect of cognition, which is sort of like only doing wrist curls in the weight room.

However, as our brain matures, it becomes less capable of processing data but much better at recognizing patterns and seeing connections. In other words, getting older can actually mean getting better at some things. This is physiologically supported by the brain applying bilaterilization (using both sides of the brain for what we used to use just one side for) and neurogenesis. These improvements may help you after middle age by creating a cognitive reserve that increases your resistance to dementia. However, it is this neurogenesis at any age that is a boon for brainpower and, potentially, innovation.

The most profound linkage between the healthy body and the creative mind is the almost mystical way in which aerobic exercise seems to literally rejuvenate and amplify problem-solving skills. I have enjoyed hitting the runner's high many, many times. About eight to ten miles into a run, the endorphins produced from exercising literally jumpstart my brain. I feel like I am on autopilot and I can just run and run and run. During these times, but even when I just do a normal three- to four-mile run of moderate intensity, I find dilemmas that were perplexing me earlier being resolved before my eyes—and feet. There were times when I was working on my PhD that the only way for me to work my way out of an analytic jam was to go for a run and then reengage with the problem.

My advice to you is to get into a habit of moderate to strenuous exercise four to five days a week; improvements to your cognitive fitness will parallel your enhanced physical fitness. It does not have to be running, but it must be deliberately a challenge and performed regularly. I know, I know … There are many brilliant, creative couch potatoes. My claim is that they could be even better if they ran around the park rather than to the cookie jar.

While physical and mental exercise is the best way to enhance cognition, it is also true that you are what you eat. The omega-3 fatty acids in fish oil may reduce depression and anxiety, while high doses might even combat Parkinson's disease. High-protein foods such as cheese, meat, and fish help generate neurotransmitters that carry messages from neuron to neuron within the brain (Habits, 2010). This so-called brain food is also good for muscle growth so that your neck can hold up that head that is housing your hundred-pound brain!

However, the single most important "food" is water. Water enables the brain and muscles to function at their highest levels since we each are around 75 percent water! Two of the first signs of dehydration are mental confusion and tiredness. Neither of these will help you create new innovative solutions.

Speaking of drinking, a simple rule that I follow that has helped a great deal in maintaining a healthy body (which serves as the platform for a creative mind) is this: do not drink your calories. This simple axiom highlights the huge health benefit that could be accrued by avoiding milkshakes, alcohol, soda, lattes, and the like. These go down so easily but still leave you craving real food. The result is that you couple high-caloric drinks with traditionally (at least for the USA) high-caloric meals, producing the great potential for overeating that leads to obesity.

In order to enhance brain function, it is important to not just *use* your brain—you must *challenge* it by providing ever-increasing stimulation in either depth (i.e., difficulty) or breadth (i.e., variety). Try to learn something new periodically or try out some new brainteasers to stimulate your mind. Get out of your comfort zone. For example, learn to say "good morning" in Russian so you can communicate with the lovely retired Russian lady who lives down the street. Learn a new Russian phrase each day or week. Challenge yourself and make a little old lady feel special.

So what small cognitive exercise will you do each Monday morning to jumpstart your brain on your drive into work? Sometimes, I look at the license plate of the car in front of me and see if it is evenly divisible by three, four, or five.

Let's say I see plate number 945EFZ. Is it divisible by three? (I then turn my head sideways as I make calculations in my head.) Yes, 315. Now, does four go evenly into the plate number? No, the plate number is not divisible by four. How about five? Yes, 189! Simple, deliberate, challenging cognitive exercises can be the foundation for fighting the creep of the aging brain and they may make a long commute pass a little more quickly.

I have mentioned my involvement earlier with a colleague in the music industry related to technology infusion. I know technology. However, music I do not know so well. I play the piano poorly and infrequently but love listening to music. That is the extent of my artistic prowess. Remember, I am a scientist, engineer, and physics professor—almost the antithesis of musical creativity. However, that did not deter me from posing a challenge to myself to write a song with my musical mentor Sterling Crew. So I have started writing one song and rearranging another one. Hopefully, these will be available at the iTunes store someday soon. It has been challenging, confusing, and rewarding. Do not be afraid to expand your cognitive horizons. Working on these songs has definitely made me use some brain cells that have lain dormant for decades.

"If you are not moving forward then you are moving backward."

—Darren McKnight

While good memory is convenient for day-to-day living, the contents of memory provide a continuous foundation for the analytical process. Whatever affects how well that information is recalled from memory will also affect the quality of the decision-making process. As a result, information really serves as the building blocks for innovation and can be stored in three ways:

- by rote (repeated verbally and in writing);

- by assimilation (new information is linked to existing knowledge); and
- using mnemonic devices (organized and encoded with a new framework, for example, an acronym).

Foundational research from the 1950s showed that no more than seven simple items (e.g., varying musical notes, subtle differences in volume, etc.) can be kept in one's head at once. This maximum level of complexity is actually smaller (about three to five items) for more complex factors such as interpretations of an engineering problem (Miller, 1956).

There is so much commonality between how you continue to improve physically as well as cognitively. I stated earlier about the importance of deliberate practice (i.e., regular and challenging activity). If you can do ten push-ups, is doing five push-ups a tough workout? No, you try to do as many as possible and then do nine push-ups in the second set. You challenge yourself. You must do the same thing cognitively.

If you do crossword puzzles that you can complete without any problem in fifteen minutes, then the research that I shared with you earlier about the lack of benefits of crossword puzzles will probably apply to you. However, if you concentrate on trying harder and harder crossword puzzles or if you try doing them faster or applying different solution techniques, then indeed you will gain cognitive benefits.

As you progress through this book from individual innovation through team-focused innovation principles and then finally to organizationally inclined precepts, you will start to see the fundamental principles that are the foundation for all innovation. These will stand out as the common themes that you can then tailor to your specific situation or challenge.

Think Outside the Box

One of the most widely used phrases for describing innovation is "think outside the box." This terminology originated from the seminal work by Kirton and has come to represent a traditional persona of creativity that no one seems to question. If you think outside the box, you are looking at a problem from a different perspective, with alternative approaches, or a varied mind-set. It is much like motherhood and apple pie. Who would question these icons? However, to be practical, it is not accurate to say that one just thinks outside the box; rather, we must look for other boxes, identify someone else's box, visit someone else's box, and then listen, learn, and bring home something from *their* box to *our* box.

> **"Innovation, the ability to conjure up genuinely new ideas without the constraints of convention or even practicality, is what will determine whether you climb along with the recovery or slide into the morass of the replaceable."**
>
> —Tom Yager

This may occur through direct interaction with individuals from those *other* boxes via exchange programs, collaborative interactions, or interdisciplinary workshops. Conversely, old-fashioned reading and research are also valuable and effective ways to gain access to other domains from which you can leverage their solutions for your own problems. One of Bill Gates' common pieces of advice is to read a book from outside of your own domain or community.

While innovation is a very personal activity, organizations often understand that not everyone can be expected to think outside the box. Organizational processes may be established where individuals are encouraged to open up the windows of their boxes and encourage flow between the boxes. This is successful when it is done in concert with the proper interpersonal guidelines such as respect for differences, normalizing inconsistent terminology, and hosting storytelling vignettes to enhance communications. In this way, an innovation catalyst stirs the pot between disparate boxes to encourage the people residing in each box to listen and learn from each other.

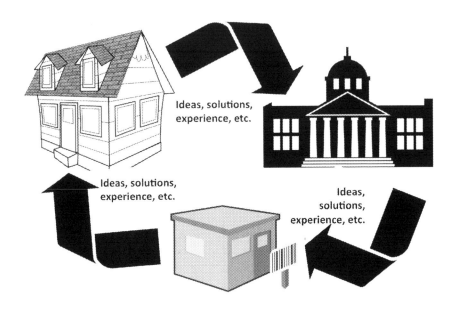

As we move forward with the newest social media and data-sharing technology, can we even talk of boxes anymore? Now we have virtual boxes much of the time, such as websites, blogs, e-books, and Facebook pages. There is hardly anything physical anymore, and the time people spend in each virtual box is getting shorter and shorter. It is almost as if we are coming down with intellectual ADD (attention deficit disorder). Simply put, we are visiting many boxes but are just flashing through them. The key is to listen, learn, and write things down when you are visiting boxes and not just race through them.

Innovation always comes back to listening and learning because, without these basic skills, each of us may be exposed to other boxes, but we will never harness the alternative approaches to improve performance within our own domain. While it sounds simple to say we should think outside the box, it requires conscious, intermediate steps of looking, visiting, listening, learning, and leveraging. For most true innovators, these steps are effortless, and they do not even recognize that they do it. For those for whom innovation is difficult, the concept of listening and learning from a foreign perspective never gets any easier and is always a real struggle.

Finally, even if you are open to listening and learning from other boxes, the efficient assimilation of this new knowledge into your problem space is nontrivial. The most likely way to capture this insight is through association or pattern recognition (i.e., genericizing the new information into a situation relevant to your domain).

This may be intellectually challenging. For example, how can the methods by which chemical processing plants maintain product quality be applied to business process workflow optimization? It is not intuitively obvious and requires some cognitive effort and skill to make such a link. Some people can do this naturally, while others need some assistance in crossing the relevance chasm between a problem in one domain and a solution in a completely different domain.

Assistance comes in the form of innovation tools (such as TRIZ, which will be covered in detail later) developed over the years and successful innovation initiatives. Proctor and Gamble's "connect and develop" strategy was an especially productive innovation catalyst that focused on collaboration.

"Think outside the box" is an oversimplification of a complex process that requires looking, visiting, listening, learning, and cognitively demanding pattern recognition to cross the relevance chasm to create true value. Some people are naturally good at both the high-touch (listening and learning) and high-tech (analytic insight required to recognize patterns) aspects of innovation. However, when they are not, organizations must both provide an environment in which developing these skills is rewarded and where individuals receive specific training to enhance interpersonal skills and learn about tools for pattern recognition.

"Imagination is more important than knowledge. Knowledge is limited."

—Albert Einstein

When I served as director of science and technology strategy at SAIC, I had a small staff that had to deal with literally thousands of technical employees. We had to be efficient and innovative about addressing our corporate responsibility to serve as the "engaged advocate for the technical workforce." I always asked people to bring to the table their own ideas about how we could do our job better.

To emphasize the openness with which I wanted to hear ideas shared, I instituted a new policy; around the holiday season in December each year, I would give everyone one extra day of vacation. However, there was a catch. They had to get a book, find a quiet place to read for eight hours, and read the book. There was no requirement as to the topic or genre of the book. However, they did have to write a half-page book report explaining how something from the book could be applied to improve team effectiveness.

I challenged them to be creative about the books they selected. One year I chose to read *Charlotte's Web* to accentuate that we can learn lessons and techniques from anyplace (someone else's box.)

"He who gains victory over other men is strong, but he who gains a victory over himself is all powerful."

—Lao Tzu

The transition from individual innovation to team innovation is not a clean break just as there are very few absolutes in innovation. However, the rule that comes closest to being absolute is that small teams (two to four people) are the sweet spot for innovation. Next I will examine enablers for team innovation.

Teams

Cognitively Diverse
Teams

Cognitive Diversity

Most great solutions do not spawn from a genius in isolation but rather from a team—but not just any team. To be successful, a team must contain and celebrate cognitive diversity. Cognitive diversity comes from having a wide array of individuals with different backgrounds, education, training, and life experiences working together in pursuit of a common cause. However, you must manage a team's potential liabilities to exploit its untapped benefits. The net result will be the cross-application of proven solutions from disparate domains, which creates powerfully creative approaches that highlight learning as the spark for innovation. This truly is the mode by which an organization can encourage its members to think outside the box.

Cognitive diversity produces several compelling benefits:

- the introduction of a variety of approaches based on a range of tools and techniques;
- the merging of disparate personal and business experiences; and
- the application of proven algorithms to new domains.

However, cognitive diversity also presents some challenges:
- Inconsistent terminology can create confusion and complicate discussions.
- Distrust may spawn from different moral and ethical foundations.
- Varied personal and cultural goals could erode teamwork.

As a result, in running a cognitively diverse team, one must be diligent in emphasizing strong communication techniques. While this process is difficult, research shows that cognitive diversity is more important than ability in many situations (Senor, 2009; Page, 2007).

"The right perspective can make a difficult problem easy."

—Scott Page

It has also been seen that having teams with members from fairly homogeneous backgrounds not only produces the minimum of skill variety but also affects how people interact. Imagine you are a young female geologist from Illinois heading to a cocktail party. As you enter the apartment, much to your surprise, every person at the party is a young female geologist from Illinois.

At first you might find it slightly amusing, but I would imagine that you would not stay long. With nothing new to learn, no interesting insights, and no intellectually exciting discoveries, there would not be a compelling reason to stay. A team with boring uniformity will also lack personal interest and group excitement in getting together. This will result in poor interactions between team members and, eventually, lackluster team performance.

Another danger in building monolithic teams is that they often pursue approaches with which they are comfortable. Just like with a crossword puzzle with an early wrong clue, it is difficult to proceed. Cognitively diverse teams have built-in safeguards against this type of cognitive bias.

"It is difficult to remove by logic an idea not placed there by logic in the first place."

—Gordon Livingston

Decision-making shortfalls will present innovation hurdles by permitting and encouraging the team to be swayed to a predetermined destination by psychological inertia or to be sabotaged by common errors. Forming and deploying cognitively diverse teams largely focuses on eliminating three types of errors that often plague team dynamics:

- anchoring error (seizing on the first bit of information that makes an impression);
- availability error (mistakenly applying memorable past events to the situation at hand); and
- attribution error (leader relying on a stereotype to which he attributes all of the project's problems).

The makeup of a team is important, but so is the size of the team and the meetings where they interact. There are general sizes of meetings or teams, and each can be associated with "people verbs" that represent what it does best:

- More than eight members: just inform and educate;
- Five to eight: inform and educate, and then act and decide
- Two to four: inform and educate to empower action and decision, and then finally learn.

It is also optimal to keep action and learning meetings to no more than an hour. Goals should be set accordingly and clearly announced at the beginning of each gathering. Informational meetings can last longer—just bring coffee!

Due to perceived problems in healthcare decision making, in 1999 a research team from Johns Hopkins examined lessons learned from high-risk industries such as air travel and nuclear energy in order to apply them to hospitals. This resulted in checks and balances being put into play. Diagnostic errors were found to be tied to shortcomings in physicians' thinking rather than technical mistakes (Groopman, 2008).

For medical imaging, interferometric synthetic aperture microscopy (ISAM) was considered to possibly provide a better means of cancer prevention by improving early tumor detection statistics. Before remote tissue imaging was possible, early detection usually necessitated invasive tumor biopsies. However, difficulties were not overcome until military synthetic aperture radar (SAR) experts applied techniques they had invented to reconstruct spatially disparate images into single high-fidelity images. This was truly a value innovation catalyzed by a cognitively diverse team (R&D, 2007).

> **"Increasingly, success at innovation requires collaboration across organizations and disciplines."**
>
> —Karim Lakhani

A culinary milestone was reached by the accidental forming of a cognitively diverse team during the 1904 St. Louis World's Fair. An ice cream vendor ran out of cups, so a Syrian waffle maker, Ernest Hami, in the neighboring booth rolled up some waffles to make cones to hold the ice cream (Page, 2007).

Thus the ice cream cone was not the result of a Fifth Avenue marketing firm's drive to increase sales of ice cream for a Fortune 500 client. It was simply the strange coincidence of neighboring booths. So, how long would it have taken for an ice cream cone to be invented without this small cognitively diverse team acting out of desperation?

This leads us to our next essay on types of innovation, in which the myriad flavors of innovation are detailed.

Types of Innovation

There are several dimensions of innovation based upon the function, motivation, and scope across which the innovation will be applied. The types of innovation based upon function start with what most people think of when they say innovation: creational innovation (i.e., making something entirely new). Creativity is the source of so many spiritual aspects of innovation.

> "To give birth to an idea—to discover a great thought—an intellectual nugget, right under the dust of a field that many a brain plow had gone over before. To find a new planet, to invent a new hinge, to find a way to make lightning carry your messages. To be first—that is the idea. To do something, say something, see something, before anybody else—these are the things that confer a pleasure compared with which all other pleasures are tame and commonplace, other ecstasies cheap and trivial."
>
> —Mark Twain

However, I have determined that while creational innovation usually deals with discovery, there are actually two ways in which creativity is manifested. The process may flow in either direction of the chain shown below:

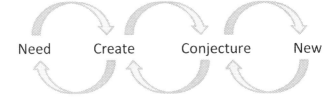

Need   Create   Conjecture   New

When the process starts with a need and then moves to the right toward a new approach this "need to new" development is considered "innovation to satisfy." This is usually associated with the process of trying to bring value to a customer. When engineers are confronted with having too many bird strikes on an airplane canopy, they must invent some device to reduce the risk from this hazard. Strengthening the cockpit is a brute-force approach that would cost a lot of money and take a lot of time. Conversely, attaching an acoustic device to the fuselage that creates a sound that birds do not like provides a creative, low-cost, and easy-to-implement solution.

But after "EUREKA!," then what? Alexander Graham Bell did not invent the telephone because he was responding to a telegraph-improvement program. He tried many different combinations of devices and triggers to create different phenomena. It is unclear if he was as interested in creating the telegraph as he was in doing something that permitted information to be passed some way other than by the physical passing of written material. He was trying to solve a problem that had not yet been identified.

The greatest innovators discover a "problem" that no one else cares about before creating a solution. By the way, many unsuccessful inventors have solved problems that have never become important. Just as I often say, "There is fine line between being overworked and unemployed," there is similarly a fine line between innovative genius and utter failure. It may be said that some of the most important creational innovations have been the result of chance: a dropped beaker in the lab that did not break; a "failed" recipe that a coworker tastes and declares the best yet; and so on.

In contrast to creational innovation, integrative innovation deals only with new combinations, not new building blocks. Integrative innovation is also the most prevalent form of innovation as it exploits legacy components of existing solutions and combines them to create new, more powerful capabilities. This recombination may manifest itself in several ways:

1. Rearrange or reorder: put the first as last, and then the last shall be first
2. Assemble or aggregate: join operationally
3. Interoperate: have two devices work together that used to work independently

4. Interface: ease the merging of two objects
5. Rediscover: dust off some old solution and apply it in a new way

Integrative innovation will become more and more important as customers want revolutionary value propositions with low risk. Integrative innovation provides the proven performance of component solutions with only the recombination being an issue. In this way, innovation will start to become more of an engineering task, creating easy interfaces that empower multiple capabilities in an orchestra of value.

Creational and integrative innovations are often discussed in terms of only technological or product innovations; however, this need not be the case. Two other types of innovation based on varying scope are process innovations (change procedure or policy) and business-model innovations (change how customers access product). Product innovation, while very popular, is also potentially higher risk and lower impact relative to process or business-model innovations.

A process innovation has medium risk and medium impact, so it is actually the sweet spot for innovation (i.e., highest expected value). It has lower risk and higher potential impact than product or technological innovation because it is easier to implement and generally has a wider scope of application within an organization. While a single technological innovation may influence those employees or customers who deal with that product, a process innovation can be applied across multiple product lines.

For example, including an iPod jack in a new automobile is truly inventive yet brings value only to iPod owners. However, the demographics of iPod users may make this modification of the automobile irrelevant to the car buyer if that model is bought by people who do not normally own iPods. On the other hand, a new automobile manufacturer permitting car buyers to finance at zero percent for the first year does not require the redesign of the dashboard of any cars and is a benefit that probably applies across a broader range of automobile buyers. As a result, the process model has the potential for better return on investment since it is appropriate for a larger number of buyers and its nonuse costs little to nothing to the dealer in sunk costs.

Business model innovation has the greatest potential impact but also the highest risk. A change in a business model potentially includes multiple innovations of both process and product types. In addition, it redefines the way in which customers interact with a business and has great potential impact yet also has great potential for failure, the reason being that if the marketplace sees the change as a move away from a critical value proposition, then the business-model innovation may fail as fantastically as it may succeed. A recent example of business-model innovation is the trend away from selling music CDs and cassettes in lieu of electronic media.

The iPod was a great technological innovation and synchronizing the device with computers to access stores of digital media files was an exceptional process innovation. However, the iPod did not really take off until the iTunes Store business innovation which made buying digital media directly online possible. The iPod was introduced in 2001, and the online iTunes Store was introduced in 2003. That is when sales of iPods really picked up for Apple.

How many of you can remember the early days of iPods when you would download a CD that you had bought at the music store and then "sync up" the iPod to move that music to the iPod. I still recall how I felt as if the world would never be the same again, but then the iTunes Store in 2003 took the CD completely out of the picture.

The last type of innovation based on scope has been practiced for years but goes by a fairly new name, open innovation. Open innovation is defined as when an entity ventures outside of its walls to engage in innovation. This has been enabled by the Internet and Web 2.0 technologies, but real innovative organizations have always looked outside through the use of consultants, advisory boards, expert panels, and the like. It is not a surprise that most organizations look to assist product development and process enhancements by using people outside of their organizations.

The current trend is toward more covert mechanisms whereby organizations look outside of their employee base for critical intellectual capital. Some are not just looking but are actually scouring every nook and cranny of the technical, business, and entrepreneurial worlds across the globe, seeking both people and solutions looking for problems. Many of the sacred aspects of research and development such as intellectual property and royalty streams are being shared or even given to partners. Sometimes this open innovation is practiced with typical partners such as universities and research labs, while more obscure partners, such as competitors, retired schoolteachers, and technology brokers, are now surfacing.

The three dimensions of innovations are mutually exclusive, but each of these has a range of potential means for implementation. The resulting number of possible innovation combinations is quite numerous and highlights the myriad forms in which an innovation may be manifested. This diversity reinforces the need to deal with fundamental innovation principles applicable to all potential situations that you can combine and tailor as needed.

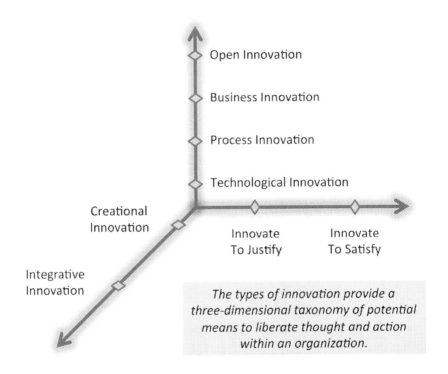

Open Innovation

Business Innovation

Process Innovation

Technological Innovation

Creational Innovation

Innovate To Justify

Innovate To Satisfy

Integrative Innovation

The types of innovation provide a three-dimensional taxonomy of potential means to liberate thought and action within an organization.

So, who is likely to execute each type of innovation? I found it useful to group people into four "innovation tendency" types according to how they execute innovation:

- Information processing (IP): speed of assimilating new information; ability to retain (i.e., remember) information; and varied modes of information processing such as aural, tactile, and visual
- Concept application (CA): ability to genericize, elaborate, and connect disparate concepts
- Intelligence quotient (IQ): ability to understand and apply complex facts
- Emotional quotient (EQ): good listening skills, tactful in team environments, and capable of putting others first

Most people have some of each of these four characteristics. However, it has been found that the ability to excel at certain types of innovations usually matches a specific combination of strengths:

- *Creational innovation* is performed by individuals who are strong in information processing and have a high intelligence quotient.
- *Integrative and open innovation* methods are practiced by those with strengths in concept application and a high emotional quotient.
- Individuals suited for *business innovation* normally have both a high intelligence and emotional quotient.
- *Process innovation* is often crafted by those skilled at information processing and concept application.
- Those proficient in concept application and with high IQs are likely to excel in *product innovation*.

These rules of thumb for innovation tendencies should be considered as flexible guidelines, not rigid requirements. However, this construct differs significantly from other rating systems for individuals that examine personality traits. The innovation tendencies are based on actual actions taken rather than how someone *feels*.

Incrementally Aggressive

Acting in an incrementally aggressive fashion is simply taking small and clear steps, early and often. Schools do not tell kindergarten students on the first day of school that they have 2,340 days of school left before they graduate from high school. When you run a marathon, the organizers do not post a sign after the first mile stating that you have 25.2 miles to go. While a final objective may be challenging and specific, there should be many intermediate points at which progress is measured and performance goals are updated, just as in any complex, challenging endeavor.

Setting goals for personal action or behavior (what you have control of), instead of targets for performance, is critical. It is important to focus on getting better at what you do (comparing your current actions against previous actions) rather than being the "best." There is always someone better, but as long as you achieve a personal best every day, then you will be inching closer to being a success.

> **"Think big and implement in little pieces."**
> —Theodore Kinni

Both of my daughters swim competitively, and the "personal best" ribbons awarded after each swim meet when they were younger were so civilized and motivational. This concept can work in the business world as well. If you challenge yourself every day to have a personal best, this seemingly unambitious goal can lead to significant progress in a short time.

While having a personal best every day or every week may not seem too difficult, it is still important to focus on *action* over thinking. You must act! Emphasize when and how you will act—and place a priority on specificity. Do not just say, "I need to improve my health by exercising more." Rather, say, "I will run every morning before I go to work." Success is based on preparation, energy, determination, and simple yet achievable goals.

An interesting mathematical riddle provides some insights into the utility of being incrementally aggressive. Imagine that there are two options for how you will get paid for a job. With the first option, you get $15,000 immediately. With the second option, you get paid over a two-week period. You get one dollar the first day, and then each day thereafter, you get double the amount you received the day before. This means that you get two dollars on the second day, four dollars on the third day, and so on until you have gotten paid daily for fourteen days. Which payment plan do you want to take? That $15,000 sounds pretty good, while getting a dollar or two and working your way up does not sound like that good of a deal. However, being incrementally aggressive and taking the second option will actually yield you over $16,000—so take that incremental payment plan.

> **"You cannot think your way into a new way of acting. You must act your way into a new way of thinking. Look for and then build upon early successes."**
>
> —Larry Bossidy

We not only execute incrementally but must also define success incrementally. By segmenting a problem or goal, you decrease the cost of failure or increase the value of failure (Hon, 2009). That is to say, it allows you to learn and recalibrate without breaking the entire sequence. You may find that you are just too sore running every day before work and so decide to alternate between running and lifting weights on a daily basis. Flexibility of action is important in being aggressive.

As long as you have not lost sight of the original general goal of improving your health, then modifying—but not eliminating—the specific actions to get there is quite acceptable and increases the chance that you will reach the ultimate goal. It is very similar to the concept of appreciative enquiry championed by the Harvard Business School; this drives one to try to find people or organizations that are "doing something right" rather than focusing on what they are doing wrong (Johnson, 2004).

It is important to keep perspective, however, by remembering to not focus on creating big winners; instead make sure that there are no big losers. One should fail early and often to be able to adjust priorities.

The purposeful act of breaking up a large activity is not only useful for minimizing the risk of getting too far off track; there is also a benefit to the morale of the individuals. Studies have shown that the intensity of a positive reinforcement is not as important as the frequency of the "warm and fuzzy." So, it is better to be told every Friday that your project completed its goals successfully and efficiently for the week than to have a single recognition at the end of the six-month effort, stating how you have been consistently on schedule and under budget. While, from my experience, this technique to enhance workforce productivity is just common sense management, it has been dubbed the Progress Principle (Amabile, 2011).

However, I have observed that this can also work against you if your incremental feedback is negative; many little nitpicky, even vague, comments can add up to erode morale much more than a single official counseling session. Do not use the power of incremental aggressiveness for evil!

"The big things are accomplished through the perfection of minor details."

—John Wooden

Being incrementally aggressive is more about seeing the general path to success and being flexible on the journey rather than following a single preordained trail to the top. Recently, I was talking to a colleague in the music industry who stated that he really needed to rejuvenate his musical production business since things were slow. I suggested that the music industry seemed like a very relationship-driven industry and that maybe an incrementally aggressive approach would be to make one phone call each day.

He could resurrect old ties, establish new ones, learn about new trends, and remind himself of his unique attributes relative to rest of the market. With no hard-sell messages and no financial quotas, he methodically reconnected with friends, colleagues, and clients. The story ends well, as this friend and I are embarking on several interesting and potentially lucrative opportunities for infusing new technologies into the entertainment industry, and he recently produced a twelve-song release for two outstanding new artists. This resurgence was partially due to his reenergized connection with his music community. As a side note, just how much more cognitively diverse can we get than combining an aerospace engineer from Washington, DC, with a musician living in San Francisco?

I am an avid yet rapidly aging runner who has run in many road races, including several marathons. People often ask me about how to get started in running, and I have a clear yet, of course, potentially counterintuitive, three-part incrementally aggressive strategy.

In Phase 1, get out of your chair and focus on time on your feet. You can walk, jog, shop, skip—I don't care. Just stay on your feet. Start at five minutes if that is all that you can do. Never increase how much time you spend on your feet by more than 10 percent per day. So, if you can do ten minutes walking, follow that up the next day with no more than eleven minutes. Eventually you will work your way up to forty-five minutes, but until then, do not worry about the distance that you are traveling. You should run as much as you can but as long as you are at least moving, you are getting your body ready.

Now you are prepared for Phase 2, during which you worry only about distance. Start with two miles of running or walking. Do not worry about the time it takes you to do the two miles, but challenge yourself to do your best. Slowly increase your mileage by no more than 10 percent *per week*. So, if you ran and walked eight miles in the first week of Phase 2, then do not exceed about 9 miles (8.8 miles) the second week. Work your way up to a five- to ten-mile total distance, depending on your eventual goal, with no consideration of the time that it takes.

Finally, in Phase 3, identify a pace goal for a certain distance and begin to refine your workouts to reach your objective. If you are not a runner and you try to start with the goal of a nine-minute-per-mile pace for a 5k race, it is unlikely that you will make it. However, if you start by looking at your *clock* (Phase 1: time on your feet), then your *map* (Phase 2: distance), and then finally at your *stopwatch* (Phase 3: focus in pace) you will reach your goal!

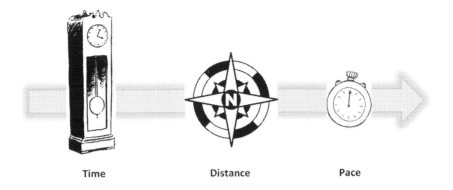

Time	**Distance**	**Pace**

I have shared this incrementally aggressive approach with colleagues who successfully transitioned from not considering themselves to be runners to finishing road races and actually enjoying them. I also applied it often when I was coaching youth track and field.

Your resume is a critical document since it is your marketing sheet. My advice to people who worked for me always was that, at the end of each year, if you could not add something significantly different or better than the year before, you had best reevaluate your current job. If your job is not challenging you enough to provide some substantive change to your resume, you either need to ratchet up your intensity or put your resume on the street. You need to consciously and regularly examine your progress, or pretty soon you will just be older—but not any better.

(Note: I have figures in my resume. I know that might sound odd, however, when doing other papers, we almost always include figures to help tell stories. Why shouldn't we do that for resumes? The comments that I got when I did this originally were very interesting and very polarized. About 75 percent of the people just loved it, but 25 percent thought that it was too different and highly recommended that I not distribute it that way. I do have two versions of my resume—one with figures and one without.)

The legacy of the written word requires that when you write any document, such as a resume, position paper, proposal, book, or final report, you must have an excellent product. Yet, it can be very daunting to figure out how to create a formidable document that you can be proud of within a reasonable timeline. An incremental approach that I have developed over the years to produce quality documents, especially when working with a team of individuals, is to reflect the four *C*'s: compliant, complete, coherent, and compelling.

- Compliant: Ensure that everyone knows exactly what is expected of the document and prepare an outline that ensures that you are doing what you are being asked to do. So often, projects are set up to fail by people who are rushing to write the content before a compliant framework has been created. Companies that respond to government requests for proposals (RFPs) often employ people whose full-time job it is to create compliance matrices that ensure that a proposal adheres to the requirements. This is not exciting work, but it is so critical to the quality of the final product.
- Complete: Now the words are put into the document. Get everyone to pour his or her heart and soul into the document, treating it sort of like written brainstorming. Do not judge individual inputs; just get the content into the document.
- Coherent: Once you have a compliant and complete document, someone needs to figure out whether or not the information flows logically and consistently. Are the sections in the best order for the reader to get the brilliance of your report or proposal? This often has to be done by someone who did not work on the first two Cs since you need to focus on logic that may be independent of the content (i.e., the context of the document).
- Compelling: Finally, the document needs to be crafted to elicit a "wow" feeling. Yes, even a technical review of the state of orbital debris in geosynchronous orbit can be made to excite the reader. This may be done in one of three ways:
- powerful graphics (not spinning paper clips but insightful data displayed expertly);
- practical analogies (e.g., equating the control of orbital debris to asbestos remediation in schools); or

- posing counterintuitive observations (e.g., the best way to remove orbital debris is to develop a solution that does not go into orbit).

This incrementally aggressive approach to creating sound written documents has served me well over the years because it allows people to do what they do best individually with a clear understanding as to how their contributions combine to craft the best possible final product. This recipe combines communication, cooperation, collaboration, and innovation for a specific task. The process is called the Innovation Value Chain (IVC) and will be discussed further later in the book. However, it is this systematic creativity that enables innovation. Order does not stifle innovation; it provides a construct that lets each person contribute to his or her fullest!

"Life is like riding a bicycle. To keep your balance you must keep moving."

—Albert Einstein

TRIZ

Have you ever sat somewhere, perplexed by a problem, and thought to yourself, "Someone else must have seen this before. What did they do?" The real question is not whether that is the case but how does someone get those proven solutions? Unfortunately, any innovative solution is really made up of two components: the fundamental innovative principle that has been applied previously and then the tailoring of that principle to a problem in a different domain.

Luckily, some poor soul with incredible patience and organizational skills saw similar patterns and spent nearly a lifetime creating a broadly applicable process to empower the crossover of existing solutions to other areas. This framework is called TRIZ (a Russian acronym for "inventive problem solving.") That lonely, patient inventor of TRIZ was a Russian patent clerk, Genrich Altshuller, who did most of his work on TRIZ in the 1940s. A key principle of TRIZ is looking for dilemmas, contradictions, unhappiness, and problems, and then resolving them in creative ways by applying solutions from other domains.

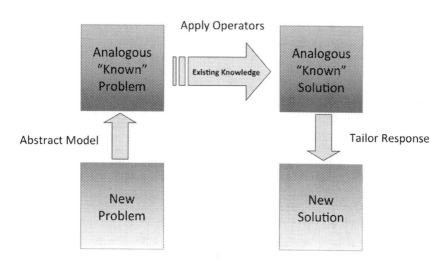

Dilemmas and contradictions are opportunities for quantum innovation. By pursuing and examining conflict, you maximize your chances to create real impactful solutions. One key aspect of this process is couching your problem in the form of a contradiction and then resolving the contradiction rather than compromising on it. This elegantly simple perspective leads to real innovation.

There are many TRIZ tools on the Internet that you can access quite easily. I took a class a few years ago from Ideation International that was very practical and allowed me to immediately apply this capability in a variety of areas. TRIZ is the epitome of systematic creativity because it provides a detailed sequence of steps in order to bring a spark from a seemingly random source to fuel problem solving in a new work dimension.

As a warning to the reader, I'll say that this is a methodology developed by an engineer for engineers. As a result, this TRIZ essay is much more technical than all the others in *Hitting the Innovation Jackpot*. I included this more technologically grounded section to provide an example of a detailed engineering innovation methodology that can be applied to very complex system problems. However, the inclusion of this more onerous lesson is also relevant, as this technical framework can be applied to very nontechnical subjects such as team dynamics, employee motivation, and so on. Without this detailed examination, you will not have the depth of understanding to apply TRIZ's fundamentals to other, nontechnical domains. Remember, as I stated earlier, you learn the most after a slight period of confusion.

Altshuller suggested that inventive problem solving could include up to four steps:

1. gathering facts about the situation to abstract a "standard" problem;
2. examining contradictions;
3. selecting relevant operators (i.e., standard solution concepts) to apply; and
4. leveraging resources.

It is the third step where most of the activities in TRIZ take place, but it is only successful when the first two steps are performed well. The fourth step provides some additional simple, useful standalone value propositions.

Gather Facts

The data needed to characterize the situation will vary widely depending on the type of problem being examined, but TRIZ identifies thirty-nine parameters that are likely going to be used to describe the functionality of the existing system and the contradictions that must be resolved in order to create an innovative solution. These physical parameters represent an extraction of decades of work by Altshuller on what information should be examined in preparing to craft a solution. The list of TRIZ physical parameters is not a magic wand. It is one man's assessment of the range of concrete variables that influence solution designs that have stood the test of time very well.

TRIZ Physical Parameters

• Weight of moving object	• Power
• Weight of non-moving object	• Waste of energy
• Length of moving object	• Waste of substance
• Area of moving object	• Waste of time
• Area of non-moving object	• Loss of information
• Volume of moving object	• Amount of substance
• Volume of non-moving object	• Reliability
• Speed	• Accuracy of measurement
• Force	• Accuracy of manufacturing
• Pressure	• Harmful factors acting on object
• Shape	• Harmful side effects
• Stability of object	• Manufacturability
• Strength	• Convenience of use
• Durability of moving object	• Repairability
• Durability of non-moving object	• Adaptability
• Temperature	• Complexity of device
• Brightness	• Complexity of control
• Energy spent by moving object	• Level of automation
• Energy spent by non-moving object	• Productivity

These physical parameters have a definite hardware flavor to them and attempts to modernize this standard terminology into realms that include more information technology have been insightful (Mann, 2003), but I personally prefer to use the original framework then to update them myself.

As discussed earlier, I feel that we are trying too hard to make everything high tech, and sometimes the legacy terminology and thoughts have that raw, unvarnished flavor that catalyzes more fundamental discussions. This is often done by taking one step back in order to take two steps forward since some of these terms may not be everyday terminology, but the extra dialogue is part of the solution process!

Examine Contradictions

After you have assembled relevant data for analysis, you will be asked to identify singularities that prevent desired or optimum performance. These fall into four categories: human and societal; interface and integrative; mechanical and logical; or business model and economic.

While not mentioned within the TRIZ process, it is clear that identifying these types of issues will require a cognitively diverse team from the onset to even recognize opportunities for innovation, much less the actual innovative solutions.

The focus then is not to perform tradeoffs but rather to resolve contradictions. There are three general principles used within TRIZ as this first filter on creative problem solving:

- *Separate contradiction in time*: A staple needs to be pointed to penetrate paper but flat to hold the papers together, so the conflict is resolved by separating its needed properties in time.
- Can you think of another innovative design that uses this principle?
- *Separate contradiction in space*: A funnel has a broad opening at one end to permit easy input of material but a small end for the exit to permit the transfer of that material into a narrow opening, so the opening-size conflict is resolved by separation in space.
- Can you think of another innovative design that uses this principle?
- *Segment or combine the contradiction*: A bicycle chain is flexible as a whole unit but rigid as an individual link. It solves the conflict of being both flexible and rigid by leveraging segmentation.

- Can you think of another innovative design that uses this principle?

This process serves to move teammates slightly out of their comfort zones by using a mental model for innovation that separates a dilemma in time, space, or form. When submariners "hot bunk" in their living quarters, this is actually a way to resolve a contradiction. There are more sailors than beds, so they resolve that contradiction by separating in time when they sleep.

Select Relevant Operators

However, application of the separation principles may not be sufficient to develop a solution; for that reason, TRIZ incorporates forty relevant operators that are considered individual solution approaches. The relevant TRIZ operators are listed below.

TRIZ Operators

- Segmentation
- Extraction
- Local Quality
- Asymmetry
- Combining
- Universality
- Nesting
- Counterweight
- Prior counter-action
- Prior action
- Cushion in advance
- Equipotentiality
- Inversion
- Spheroidality
- Dynamicity
- Partial or overdone action
- Moving to a new dimension
- Mechanical vibration
- Periodic action
- Continuity of a useful action

- Rushing through
- Convert harm into benefit
- Feedback
- Mediator
- Self-service
- Copying
- Inexpensive, short-lived object for expensive, durable one
- Replacement of a mechanical system
- Pneumatic or hydraulic construction
- Flexible membranes or thin film
- Use of porous material
- Changing the color
- Homogeneity
- Rejecting and regenerating parts
- Transformation of the physical and chemical states of an object
- Phase transformation
- Thermal expansion
- Use strong oxidizers
- Inert environment
- Composite materials

Within the TRIZ framework, each of these operators (i.e., inventive principles) are clearly defined. For example the full definition for asymmetry (the fourth one in the first column) is "replace a symmetrical form with an asymmetrical form. If an object is already asymmetrical, increase the degree of asymmetry. *Example:* Make one side of a tire stronger than the other to withstand impact with the curb."

The relevant operator is selected from the contradiction matrix based upon the contradiction discovered from the problem statement. The full contradiction matrix is necessarily a thirty-nine-by-thirty-nine matrix, with the rows and columns being the thirty-nine physical parameters used to describe the contradiction between two factors. The entries in each cell are the inventive principles that might be useful in creating a new, innovative solution. The complete contradiction matrix can be downloaded from http://www.triz40.com/aff_Matrix.htm.

A simple scenario, from the Ideation International training, examines how to make a cannon smaller and more mobile. The barrel of a cannon is considered the nonmoving object and the projectile (or shot) is the moving object. To eject the shot, there must be sufficient pressure while the shape and stability of both objects are maintained, which implies strength of both. To make the cannon small, we strive to reduce both the area and volume of both the cannon barrel and the shot.

An exhaustive analysis may highlight many more parameters to be considered, but if we look at a subset of the contradiction matrix we can see several potential relevant operators in the cells of the table that hint at potential inventive principles to apply in the solution process. To show the relationships between the system parameters and performance requirements, a partial contradiction matrix (four by four) tailored just for our limited, specific scenario is created.

Partial Contradiction Matrix

	5. Area : Moving Object	6. Area : Non-Moving Object	7. Volume: Moving Object	8. Volume: Non-moving Object
11. Pressure	10, 15, 28, 36	10, 15, 36, 37	6, 10, 35	24, 35
12. Shape	4, 5, 10, 34	-	4, 14, 15, 22	2, 7, 35
13. Stability	2, 11, 13	39	10, 19, 28, 39	28, 34, 35, 40
14. Strength	3, 29, 34, 40	9, 28, 40	7, 10, 14, 15	**9, 14, 15, 17**

If we then decide to focus on resolving the contradiction that we must maintain strength (parameter 14) while preventing the volume of the nonmoving object (parameter 8) from increasing, then the matrix identifies four inventive principles to consider as seen in the lower right-hand corner of the partial contradiction matrix:

- 9. Prior Counter-Action: Perform a counteraction in advance by possibly reinforcing the shaft made from several pipes that have been previously twisted to some specified angle.
- 14. Spheroidality – Curvature: Instead of using rectilinear parts, use curved parts. For example, use arches to eliminate stress concentrations that might lead to failure.
- 15. Dynamics: Make an object flexible if it used to be rigid, by letting some component bend and thus allowing it to withstand greater loads.
- 17. Moving to a New Dimension: Use a multilayered assembly of objects instead of a single layer. An example would be a greenhouse that has a concave reflector on the northern part of the house to improve illumination of that part of the house by reflecting sunlight during the day.

Leverage Resources

While the application of the contradiction matrix hints at possible ways to resolve contradictions, TRIZ also identifies leveraging resources as a way to develop innovative solutions. First, perform an inventory of the resources available. These may be either readily available or derived. These resources, as outlined in Ideation International training, can be categorized as follows:

- Functional: A system or its surroundings may be able to perform other functions.
- Fields: Mechanical, thermal, chemical, electrical, kinetic, magnetic, and electromagnetic energies and actions may be usable as part of solving performance issues.
- Information: Context available due to the functioning of the system may be exploited.
- Space: Volume in or around the component being analyzed may be used to enhance performance.
- Substances: Material in the system or its surroundings can be leveraged.
- Time: Increments of time before, during, or after the technological process examined may be used to your advantage.

Sometimes when the resource is not directly available, you may have to craftily create the needed resource by manipulating your surroundings. A great example of this occurred in 1903 when a steamship on a German polar expedition got stuck in the ice. The crew was two kilometers from open water, and the sailors could not break through the ice, even with the help of explosives. The temperature was well below freezing, the ship was trapped in ice, and food was running low. What could the crew do?

The predicament was solved by using furnace ash, which the sailors poured onto the ice. The dark ash absorbed the energy of the bright polar sun and melted a path through the ice. The desperate crew transformed the sunlight resource and black ash to create the ice-melting function needed to break loose of the polar ice.

In a more modern example, recent research at Harvard has examined the synergy of waste in manufacturing processes. Typically, manufacturing plants have a requirement to minimize waste. However, analysis has shown that depending on the type and amount of waste, it might be beneficial overall to create more waste if it is possible to treat it as a resource that can be consumed or distributed to bring additional value to the business dynamic. This may even be advantageous as the relaxing of waste-production controls makes the original process much more efficient (Blanding, 2011).

Another intriguing example of innovation that follows the framework of TRIZ (though it occurred well before the methodology was created by Altshuller) is depicted in the book by Dava Sobel, *Longitude*. Sobel describes the amazing feats of engineering and innovation required to conquer the high seas in the 1700s while providing several TRIZ-like innovations.

The crux of the problem Sobel describes was determining a reliable way to calculate the longitude of a ship when it was nowhere near a geographic landmark. The primary approach of the time was to use star and planet location to determine a ship's longitude. The major deficiency was that timekeeping was very imprecise and the environment on the ships made it very difficult for any clock to function accurately and reliably. The salt and moisture combined with the temperature extremes and rough conditions of the open seas made any clock of that time very unreliable.

John Harrison, a clockmaker, knew that the first issue to overcome was to create tough gears within a clock that would not require constant lubrication. The normal metal gears were strong enough but they rusted easily, while traditional wooden gears were not tough enough. So in a typical TRIZ-like moment (though Mr. Harrison obviously had never heard of the approach), he considered how he could resolve the contradiction of having gears that were both tough but that would also not rust.

His solution was ingenious. He cut wood gears so that the grain made the gears tough enough (the lines of the grains of wood radiated from the center of the gear), and he used a type of wood (a tropical hardwood called lignum vitae) that "exudes its own grease," which served as a lubricant with no chance for the gears rusting. He applied a TRIZ principle of leveraging available resources by using this naturally produced lubricant that came from the wood for the gears.

Another problem for at-sea clocks was the movement affecting the pendulum used for the timing of a clock. The pendulum must maintain a constant length to keep time accurately but, again, must also be tough. The toughness quality could only be met by using metal for the pendulum.

However, metal is greatly affected by changes in temperature causing the pendulum to change in length drastically. When it was colder the pendulum would contract, making the clock run faster; when it got warmer, the pendulum elongated, and the clock ran more slowly.

The contradiction was there again staring John Harrison straight in the face. The pendulum must be tough but not be adversely affected by changing temperatures. The first option of using wood failed for the same reason as before, lack of toughness. However, Mr. Harrison noted that different metals had significantly different coefficients of thermal expansion (which meant that different metals were affected differently by changes in temperature). So what? How could that help? Harrison noted that if he made a pendulum out of two types of metal with different coefficients of thermal expansion, then the pendulum would actually keep a constant length as the two metals counteracted their respective tendencies. This approach is clearly stated within TRIZ as "using a counter-force to an unwanted action," but John Harrison just did this all by himself, trying to win a competition prize (Sobel, 1995).

The magic of TRIZ is the application of a repeatable methodology whereby any problem is characterized by the resolution of a technical contradiction. That technical contradiction has a subset of operators identified as being potentially advantageous to the problem being studied. This approach basically captures the knowledge generalized from Altshuller through reviewing tens of thousands of patent applications and categorizing his findings into principles that can be applied to any domain.

I personally applied TRIZ to a complex oceanographic system problem. The resulting operator that was suggested to potentially apply in managing the future costs of a large-scale buoy network was called nesting. This inventive principle implied that standardizing the construction of up to six to eight different-sized buoys needed for varying sea conditions by nesting a common, central payload within a series of interchangeable shells would greatly reduce costs without impacting performance. This innovative approach was recognized as one of the technical features that led to the selection of our proposal.

Innovation by Axiom

Innovation by axiom is simply the application of quotes or one-liners as a means to inspire people to perform in innovative, positive ways. In marketing, this is often considered branding, whereby a provider explains briefly and ingeniously to a product's consumers a message that embodies a differentiating value in a simple, memorable statement. Sound communication expedites innovation and helps to create a shared vision. Below I have presented some of the best lists and one-liners that have proven to be powerful and convincing as standalone axiomatic enablers. It is doubtful that any list or collection will apply "as is" to your needs, but examine how these are formed and make your own!

> **"Get enough monkeys in a barrel, and they will eventually write *King Lear*."**
>
> —Garrick Utley

The creative enigmas of Heraclitus are some of the first of these sorts of insights that, while general in nature, can be used to provide very specific solutions or at least create the energetic curiosity needed to solve problems. Read these selected enigmas carefully; they are packed full of interesting insights and useful summaries for action (Von Oech, 2001).

A wonderful harmony is created when we join together the seemingly unconnected.

Knowing many things doesn't teach insight.   Everything flows.

The cosmos speaks in patterns.   Expect the unexpected, or you won't find it.

The Creative Enigmas of Heraclitus

If all things turned to smoke, the nose would become the discerning organ.

A thing rests by changing.   When there is no sun, we can see the evening stars.

Dogs bark at what they don't understand.   You can't step into the same river twice.

More recently, Charles Sykes provided a great list of items about life and problem solving for high school graduates to consider as they enter the working world and that are relevant to anybody ranging from high school graduates to retirees. This list is often erroneously cited as being penned by others for a high school graduation speech in 2005 (Sykes, 1996).

"11 Things They Did Not Learn in High School"
By Charles Sykes

1. **Life is not fair** – get used to it.
2. **The real world won't care about your self-esteem.**
    The world will expect you to accomplish something BEFORE you feel good about yourself.
3. You will NOT make $60,000 a year right out of high school.
    You won't be a vice-president with a car phone until you earn both.
4. If you think your teacher is tough, **wait until you get a boss**.
5. Flipping burgers is not beneath your dignity.
    Your grandparents had a different word for burger flipping. They called it opportunity.
6. If you mess up, it's not your parents' fault, so **don't whine** about your mistakes, learn from them.
7. Before you were born, your parents weren't as boring as they are now.
    They got that way from paying bills, cleaning your clothes and
        listening to you talk about how cool you thought they were.
8. Your school may have been done away with winners and losers, but life HAS NOT.
    In some schools they have abolished failing grades as they'll give you as MANY TIMES as you want to get the right answer.
        This doesn't bear the slightest resemblance to ANYTHING in real life.
9. Life is not divided into semesters. **You don't get summers off and very few employers are interested in helping you FIND YOURSELF.** Do that on your own time.
10. **Television is not real life.**
    In real life people actually have to leave the coffee shop and go to jobs.
11. Be nice to nerds. Chances are you'll end up working for one.

Google is seen as the prototypical innovative organization. This high-tech company has rules to live by, and interestingly they all deal with people (high touch), not technology (Newsweek, Dec 2005).

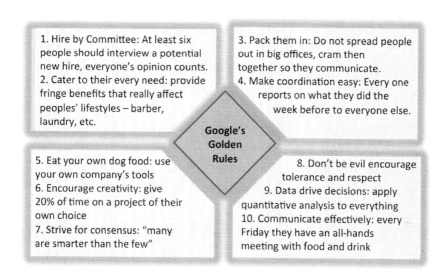

1. Hire by Committee: At least six people should interview a potential new hire, everyone's opinion counts.
2. Cater to their every need: provide fringe benefits that really affect peoples' lifestyles – barber, laundry, etc.

3. Pack them in: Do not spread people out in big offices, cram then together so they communicate.
4. Make coordination easy: Every one reports on what they did the week before to everyone else.

Google's Golden Rules

5. Eat your own dog food: use your own company's tools
6. Encourage creativity: give 20% of time on a project of their own choice
7. Strive for consensus: "many are smarter than the few"

8. Don't be evil encourage tolerance and respect
9. Data drive decisions: apply quantitative analysis to everything
10. Communicate effectively: every Friday they have an all-hands meeting with food and drink

Apple has a similar if not even more prominent reputation as being eerily simple in its innovativeness. Apple has seven core values that have served the company well and might do the same for you (Breen, 2011).

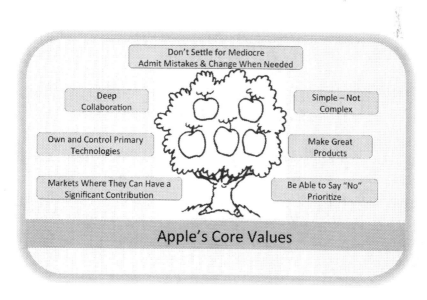

Don't Settle for Mediocre
Admit Mistakes & Change When Needed

Deep Collaboration

Simple – Not Complex

Own and Control Primary Technologies

Make Great Products

Markets Where They Can Have a Significant Contribution

Be Able to Say "No" Prioritize

Apple's Core Values

While these previous lists are powerful, I have a few one-liners that, while even more concise, may have far-reaching application and utility for you and your organization.

> **"The average is never right. It is high half of the time and low half of the time."**
>
> —Darren McKnight

Clearly this is not absolutely true, but it does provide insights and instruction well beyond the few words used. This axiom encourages people to release the importance of the average when it comes to decision making. The average may never occur, much less even be the most likely outcome. In analyzing real-world situations, it is more often the variability of data that drives how events will unfold (e.g., what is the worst possible outcome versus what is the most typical event).

By the way, the most likely outcome is the median and is usually most relevant when the data is in integer chunks, for example, the number of free throws someone can make in a row. Having an average of 3.90 is meaningless for two reasons. First, no one can make 0.90 of a free throw. Second, an average of 3.90 implies that four free throws is the real rounded average, and people might suggest that that is the most likely event—but it may not be. A set of free throw data for eleven trials (in which someone attempts to make as many free throws as possible out of five attempts) is 0, 0, 4, 4, 5, 5, 5, 5, 5, 5, 5.

This data results in an average of 3.90 free throws made. However, the median (the most likely occurrence) is five, so that the average (even rounded) is not even the most likely event.

The power of using an innovation axiom is to remind people of a business or solution framework without having to explain all of the details. You should use axioms to remind yourself of guiding principles without having to explain the entire logic chain. Axioms are often shorthand for more expansive mental models. I just showed you the math above to provide some context, but if that much explanation is needed, then the axiom probably will not hold anyone's attention. Therefore, I use that axiom only in crowds that I am sure will get the difference between mean and median.

> **"Most engineering problems spawn out of people not understanding the difference between precision and accuracy."**
>
> —Darren McKnight

Again, this mathematically rooted axiom suggests that a critical eye toward facts and their context is necessary for solid decision making or innovative exchanges. It implies that describing something in great detail means that you know a lot about. However, that may not be true.

Saying that there were forty-four shoppers in the parking lot suggests that you have resolved the crowd down to the individual. However, if there were really fifteen shoppers present, you would have been highly inaccurate—but very precise. This is not a great combination, but it happens more often than you might think.

> **"At BASF, we don't make a lot of the products you buy. We make a lot of the products you buy better."**
>
> —BASF corporate web site

This is a brilliant brand and clear value proposition. This statement provides BASF with the foundation to develop and deploy many advanced technologies that have propelled it into an $80 billion-per-year behemoth. It is brilliant for BASF to say that they do not make products themselves, rather, they simply make what other people produce better. You always need somebody else's product to be better. Now, if I said BASF was a chemical company, would you even know what that meant and would you be as intrigued with the possibilities as you were with the "make other products better" approach? This axiom helps you understand the importance of selling or focusing on what you *do* to provide value to a customer or colleague and not what you *are*. As I discussed earlier, it is more important to focus on doing over being.

"Listen, learn, and write things down!"

—Darren McKnight

This simple axiom is my favorite saying, and I covered it earlier in the book but felt it needed another shout-out as an innovation axiom. It reflects key issues for a professional services provider, exceptional engineering support, quality assistant coach, responsive academic department, and a myriad of other roles and areas. This mantra uses people verbs so you know exactly what to do. It does not explain why. Just do it! Some actions are so pure and explicit that they rarely steer you astray.

Sometimes, I say, "Listen, learn, and leverage," for alliterative purposes, but it is not as clear since leveraging is not as meaningful as "write things down." However, "leverage" does hint at the potential benefit of listening and learning.

"Innovation framework: stay relevant, solve real-world problems in simple ways, and remember that research is part of a team."

—Robert Buderi

Robert Buderi, in his book *Engines of Tomorrow*, described his unified theory of innovation with this simple saying. While it is not complete as an innovation methodology, it is indeed coherent and compelling. These carefully selected words produce an implementable and exciting approach to almost any endeavor, and given your situation, these may resonate better with your organization than pages of policies. Set the vision and then let the policies and procedures evolve in ways that are consistent with that understandable vision.

"Innovation by Axiom" is the logical essay to transition to the "Organizations" section of this book. Many of these axioms are complete enough to be the foundation for success and productivity of an entire organization, as for Google and Apple. The following essays for organizational innovation aggregate many of the principles detailed thus far in the book. As I discussed early, the ability to get an entire organization excelling in all dimensions of execution requires attention at all levels: individuals, teams, and organizations. If you can enable innovation orchestrated at all levels you will be much more likely to hit the innovation jackpot.

Organizations

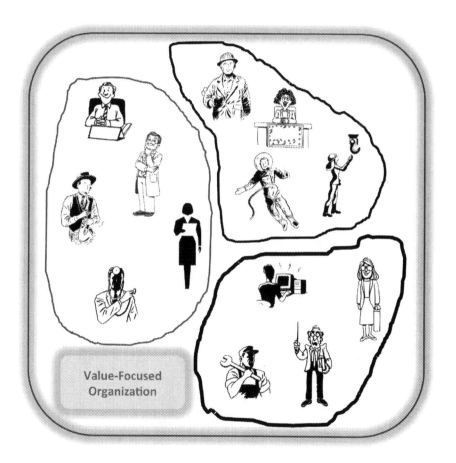

Value-Focused Organization

Maslow's Hierarchy of Needs for the Twenty-First-Century Workforce

Maslow's hierarchy of needs is a classic presentation of priorities of human needs (Maslow, 1943). This construct was formulated in the 1940s, and while I do not question the efficacy of this paradigm for humans, many of us in the industrialized world are well provided for and quite content in all dimensions of basic human needs. So the real question is how do we combine this ageless framework to help motivate a twenty-first-century workforce and encourage innovation?

These needs are cumulative. For example, a person does not look to satisfy esteem needs without already being secure in physiological, security, and team "belongingness" dimensions.

Family of Needs	How to Satisfy Need
Physiological	Health, sleep, and time
Security	Job security and organizational existence (self)
Belongingness	Team spirit, teamwork, organizational culture linkage between self and others)
Esteem	Fairness and accountability (linkage between activities and rewards)
Self-Actualization	Deep association with the organization

The five families of needs prescribed by Maslow provide a useful continuum for basic human needs and means to satisfy them. However, for the twenty-first-century employee, it is critical to understand what operational levers might be available to companies to provide organizational support to enhance productivity and innovativeness of typical workers. The figure below identifies potential ways to deal with subsets of a twenty-first-century workforce. One motivator will likely not work for all people, yet even this construct may be overly constraining since not all members of an organizational strata think the same way.

The new potential drivers are overlaid with the twenty-first-century organization hierarchy:

- *Awareness* of good work is often the most important incentive. Just a hearty "atta boy" is sufficient for many. Yes, high touch is important to our high-tech employees!

- *Procedural or policy changes*, plus vision and mission refinement, are some of the most foundational ways to inspire manual workers, analysts, and engineers. This shows the feeling that workers want to be able to influence their surroundings to make a difference in their organization's future. Employees want to see actions, not just hear words.

- *Training* is a strategic investment that many workers would prefer over money since it will likely bring increased salaries in the future. Similar to compound interest, education builds value over time.

- *Counseling* is useful for those workers who want to excel but are not sure how, and it still represents an investment by the organization into the employee.

- Most executives at the highest levels are not really concerned with training and autonomy any longer. They are already highly qualified and have sufficient autonomy, leaving largely *financial incentives* as a useful lever for motivation. For middle and upper management, the incentives are more limited, yet the desire to have an impact on the organization is still paramount. The organizational changes requested by these workers are as much for creating new leadership opportunities as they are for a feeling of autonomy.

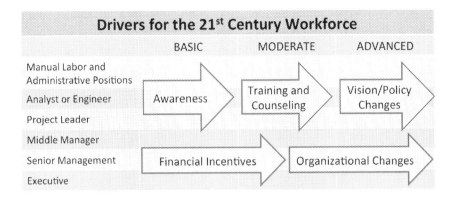

A complementary approach to the same issue (i.e., employee motivation) was taken by professors at the Harvard Business School who identified critical personal needs that motivated employees. They found that modern workers had four primary drives: to acquire, to bond, to understand, and to defend.

The *drive to acquire* was best satisfied by recognizing good behavior but also by highlighting the difference between acceptable performance and what was not acceptable. It seems that the modern worker understands that the appraisal "everyone is doing a great job" is the sign of lazy management, unable or unwilling to identify poor behavior.

The *drive to bond* is best satisfied by changing the work environment through focusing on teamwork and collaboration. This is often manifested by the sharing of best practices and discussions about how to implement these as a group.

The *drive to understand* is reinforced by better segmentation of the workflow within an organization, with individual roles clearly defined. The enhanced understanding of one's role in an organization also must emphasize the importance of each worker's position to the overall organization.

Lastly, some workers have a *drive to defend* their worth. This requires implementation of performance management and resource allocation processes to build trust among the workers (Nohria, 2008).

The most important facet related to how we address motivating teams is that we really cannot *do* anything to someone else to motivate them. That does not scale well. How long do you have to stimulate a worker to keep him or her interested? Your job is to create an environment or culture that inspires people to work with passion on jobs that they feel are important.

An organization's culture is not an ethereal cloud of magic. Culture is created through a sequence of purposeful actions that reinforce positive behavior. The deliberate act to permit people to have autonomy and flexibility is a spark for creating a value-focused culture because it shows that the organization does indeed care about the individuals. I often tell people that stress does not come from being overworked, it comes from lack of control!

So, let your employees know that the future of the organization is largely based on their actions and that you are seriously considering their inputs on how the organization is run and be sure to provide ample opportunities for training. The result will be an employee base that will work hard and remain loyal!

East versus West

The compass designed and used by the Chinese (developed independently of the European compass) has its prime direction pointing south, the opposite of the north-pointing European compass (Turner, 2011). The reflective congruence between Eastern and Western thought, epitomized by this interesting contrast, is an intriguing platform for discussion about innovation.

Many Western scholars have examined the evolution of mankind since the beginning of time and hypothesized that we have transitioned from stage to stage: agricultural age leads to industrial age leads to information age leads to conceptual age, for instance. This truly is a Western outlook to highlight differences in cultural priorities sufficient to distinguish independent eras. Eastern philosophers focus, conversely, on similarities between ages, highlighting common features. Their goal of social analysis is to identify how laws of social interaction are universally constant, unifying, and absolute.

In examining the East versus the West philosophically, ancient China and Greece can be considered as exemplars of these extremes. Over two thousand years ago in China, Confucius and Tao exemplified the ideal state in which two opposing but mutually supporting worlds peacefully coexist. Taoism focused on the yin (the feminine, dark, passive) alternating with the yang (masculine, light, and active). This relationship that exists between two opposing but interpenetrating forces that may complete one another, make each comprehensible, or create the conditions for altering one another is opposite of the deterministic Western stance. Confucianism states that an individual works, not for self-benefit, but for the entire family.

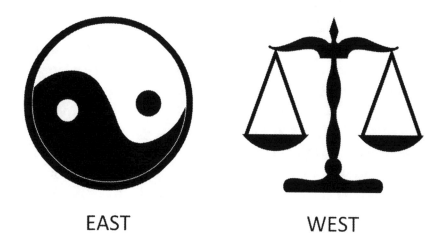

EAST   WEST

Eastern thought focuses on unifying themes and belief in constant change, with the world always moving back to some prior state. This equilibrium appreciates the middle ground that Western thinkers often consider to be a compromising of values. The typical Easterner cannot understand the part without understanding the whole. They search for relationships between things rather than categorizing as Westerners often are inclined to do. As a result, the Eastern thinker is able to handle ambiguity better and considers the context of an argument (i.e., the associated environment), which may, unfortunately, make them more susceptible to "hindsight bias" (a belief that they knew it all along).

Eastern philosophy also emphasizes fixing a problem over finding the source of the problem. This makes Eastern medicine typically much more focused on body-wise prevention, while the West retains the analytic, object-oriented, and interventionist approaches where the offending part is removed or altered. The East is far more holistic and until very recently did not consider surgery to be a reasonable medical option since it focused unduly on a single cause of disease. Eastern thought purports that good health stems from a balance of favorable forces in the body while disease is caused by a complex set of forces. These complex dynamics should be met by equally complex, usually natural, remedies and preventives (Nisbett, 2003).

Easterners are more likely to notice important situational factors and to realize that they play a role in producing behavior. As a result, they are less likely to fall victim to fundamental attribution error, which is basically putting too much emphasis on a single attribute of an individual (versus the aggregate contextual situational factors). Americans' contradiction phobia may sometimes cause them to become more extreme in their judgments under conditions in which the evidence indicates they should become less extreme.

Conversely, Easterners have a greater preference for compromise solutions and for holistic arguments, and they are more willing to endorse both of two apparently contradictory arguments. We need to be careful not to assume motive when they do this. We might generally think that, when an Easterner does this, the individual is trying to deceive us as to what he or she really will do, when in fact the person is merely reflecting his or her appreciation for flexibility (in advance).

Even how Easterners and Westerners interpret the exact same information is a function of their general cultural tendencies. A classic grouping exercise has a picture of three items: a cow, a chicken, and grass. Which of the two items, the chicken or the grass, goes with the cow?

Westerners mostly said the chicken since it was an animal like the cow (i.e., the same type of object). Easterners primarily said the grass; since a cow eats grass, they are related by what they do. The Westerners focused on categories of items while Easterners focused on relationships between items.

Western thought on information is more segregative and emphasizes living in a more deterministic world with a focus on objects or people instead of a larger, unified picture. As a result, Westerners believe more that they can control events because they know the rules that govern the behavior of objects. Ancient Chinese believed that cosmic events such as comets and eclipses could predict important occurrences on Earth, such as the birth of conquerors. But when they discovered the regularities in these events, rather than building models of them, they lost interest in them.

Alternatively, Greeks thrived on trying to correlate events with a given model and then refining that model to account for all of the objects being considered and to describe the role of each component cleanly. The Chinese were right about the importance of the field in the understanding of the behavior of the object and they were right about the complexity, but their lack of interest in categories prevented them from discovering laws that really were capable of explaining classes of events. Greeks tended to oversimplify and to be satisfied by generalizations involving nonexistent properties of objects; but they correctly understood the necessity to categorize objects in order to apply rules to them.

Lack of curiosity was characteristic of China. There was never a strong interest in knowledge for its own sake. They were more interested in the pragmatic application of knowledge over abstract theorizing. Galileo and Newton made their discoveries partially because of their curiosity and critical habits of mind, especially public debate (Nisbett, 2003).

While Westerners emphasize creational innovation (i.e., individual over the organization), Easterners find no weakness in being a fast follower. This approach has served Chinese and Japanese industries well over the last decades as Americans have created new fads, products, or styles; soon thereafter, though, the mass production of these items have almost invariably ended up in the East.

Eastern culture, while unifying of technical concepts, still has a forced, segregative approach to interpersonal relationships. This is often mentioned as a reason for lack of international scientific accomplishment. It is theorized that the extreme deference given to elders and the lack of support for young researchers to question superiors makes innovative breakthroughs difficult.

So, in general, it can be said that Easterners attempt to unify on content but segregate or partition on context (i.e., interpersonal relationships). Western culture appears to do the exact opposite. We applaud the unifying of our social interactions. It is seen as highly desirable that we speak as frankly and honestly with our boss as we do to the grocery clerk. Simultaneously, Westerners strive to partition data and "rack and stack" causes as discussed earlier. So all in all, Western thought unifies on context but segregates on content.

	Content Data Constructs	Context Personal Constructs
West	**SEGREGATE**	Unify
East	Unify	**SEGREGATE**

In the future, the two worlds of East and West will either converge with fewer extremes and more hybrid East/West people or the East and West stances will stay distinct and even continue to diverge. However, if the two worlds become indistinct, will the final state be more Western or more Eastern? It appears that many countries are becoming Westernized as children in Japan, China, Russia, and other countries are wearing US jeans, jerseys from US sports teams, and so on. However, simultaneously, some Western cultures have embraced Eastern mind-sets of business and philosophy.

Convergence of Eastern and Western thinking and culture has been occurring for many years in medicine, education, parenting, and other areas. Europe is almost a classic hybrid culture in many ways already. East and West may contribute to a blended world where social and cognitive aspects of both cultures are represented but transformed. For example, the individual ingredients in a stew are recognizable but are altered as they affect the whole.

I believe that superior performance in the future will be led by those who can alternate between Western and Eastern thinking, as needed. This holistic assessment may make it sound as if I am trying to be politically correct; however, the reality is that every situation is different, so the optimal solution methodology will depend on the context. However, this appreciation of both Eastern and Western approaches is arguably an Eastern perspective at heart.

Reverse Innovation

When you play the Beatles' song "I'm So Tired" backward, do you hear the line "Paul is dead?" Backmasking is the playing of sounds backward for a variety of purposes. Indeed, the Beatles used recordings of musical instruments played backward to produce unique sounds though it is highly questionable that they laced their songs with obtuse messages via backmasking.

> **"When you have only a hammer everything looks like a nail."**
>
> —Abraham Maslow

When trying to find your way through a maze, do you have any tricks? How about going in the reverse direction? It is always easier.

Have you ever tried to put together a bicycle or gas grill and been completely confused until you went to the end of the instructions and then followed the instructions backward?

I imagine many of you have experienced something similar in at least one scenario. Reverse imaging, reverse recording, reverse logic, and yes, even reverse innovation are all viable techniques to provide insight and overcome mental hurdles.

In the product world, taking an existing solution and searching for a new application has been quite beneficial in the past. The inventors of the SpinPop were looking for a better product to capitalize on their technology solution (a small motor at the bottom of a lollipop). After wandering through the aisles at Wal-Mart, they came up with the idea of an inexpensive electric toothbrush as the challenge needing a solution. The Spinbrush became the most popular toothbrush in America and in less than four years grew a $1.5 million investment into a $475 million sale to Proctor and Gamble. Their fate was secured by identifying the right nail for their hammer (Nalebuff, 2003).

The USA National Innovation Marketplace, at the Planet Eureka site, enables an inventor to offer a solution to subscribers who may use it to solve their own problems or, even possibly, invest in the idea to productize it for general consumption. As one might imagine, electronic communications and social media have taken the process of a solution trying to find a problem to an entirely new scale.

Planet Eureka was established by Eureka Ranch Technologies, a firm that specializes in innovation, leadership, and marketing training. Planet Eureka attempts to couple businesses that get to view inventors' concepts for one hundred days before they are made available to all subscribers (McGee, 2008).

However, Planet Eureka is not the first website to serve as an innovation marketplace. InnoCentive (a spin-off of Eli Lilly) and NineSigma have been helping companies find solutions to business needs for years. The difference is that Planet Eureka put the inventors in charge, allowing them to post concepts for people and companies to review.

The inventors and potential investors do not even pay to use Planet Eureka. The company charges for the services it provides inventors with, such as workshops on how to maximize the likelihood of garnering a buyer.

On average, InnoCentive offers up a new challenge every day and solves one every three days. The Oil Spill Recovery Institute, a group Congress formed to develop techniques to deal with oil spills, asked InnoCentive for help. The result was a resounding success that paired them with a concrete specialist who recommended a process that separates oil from water through vibrations and that is facilitated by the oil and water both being frozen.

The inventor (the solution provider) earned $20,000 for his recommendation. InnoCentive charges a fixed fee to post a problem and then also receives a commission on the fee paid to the solution provider. One of the key success factors of InnoCentive is presenting challenges to experts in domains other than the ones in which the problems originated. This leverages the concept of cognitive diversity on a problem-solving team contributing to innovative solutions.

NASA has leveraged InnoCentive on a regular basis to get breakthrough insights on everything from biological processes for astronauts to modeling future solar activity.

Reverse innovation is really just an offshoot of TRIZ without the analytic tracing between the existing solution and the current problem. Simply exposing creative solutions to an audience provides, at a minimum, opportunities to learn. It looks very similar to TRIZ in reverse.

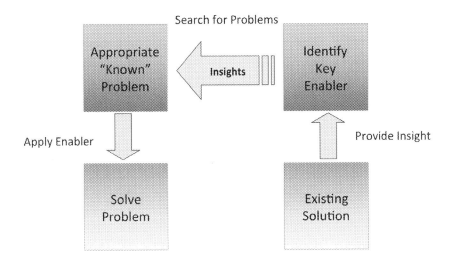

Reverse innovation may, potentially, supply a specific solution to a challenging problem with much less work than if the problem owner toiled to solve it within his or her own community. This is a different way to benefit from cognitive diversity without dealing with many of the liabilities.

Notice as we examine these organizational innovation frameworks that they all include multiple applications of topics discussed earlier in the book for individual and team innovation. If your organization is built of individuals who have read this book, your organizational innovation initiative will be more successful.

Innovation Value Chain

In 2004, while serving as director of science and technology strategy of SAIC, I established the Innovation Value Chain (IVC), which prescribes activities required to enhance workforce productivity and enable innovative technical operations (Harris, 2007). A critical theme permeating the IVC is that all four of its phases —communicate, cooperate, collaborate, and innovate—are performed by people.

> **"Innovation without focus equates to a loss of productivity. Productivity without innovation equates to a loss of quality."**
>
> —Thad Scheer

Therefore, in any approach to enhancing organizational performance, one must use people verbs (i.e., actions that people take, not activities that organizations do). For example, when asked to align their efforts with strategic objectives, it is difficult to expect that people will know what behavior will satisfy this policy. However, if they are told to "listen, learn, and write things down when attending interdepartmental meetings," they have clear actionable behavior to model.

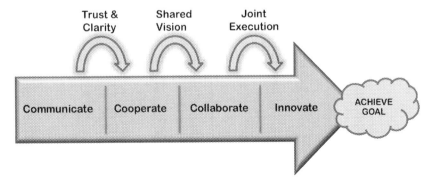

The Innovation Value Chain provides a logical sequence of people-centric activities to empower organizational effectiveness in attaining strategic goals.

When applying the IVC, it is important to first establish a clear, relevant, achievable, and challenging goal. This provides a common motivation for all other activities, accountability for all constituents, and a metric for success.

"If you don't know where you are going, you will end up somewhere else."

—Yogi Berra

Finding your bull's-eye or desired result is the first step in any attempt to harvest innovation within your organization. You have to know what your goal is if you hope to achieve it. This objective should be value-based, measurable, and simple. Just as important, it must be memorable so that participants can internalize the destination of the process. If you do not know where you are going, you either will never get there, or success will be defined as where you are when you run out of energy.

Communicate

Once the goals are established, the sequence of people-centric activities of the IVC begins. Communicating expectations, motivations, and aspirations in a memorable way for all constituents is critical to success. The "communicate" figure outlines actions performed and products resulting from this stage.

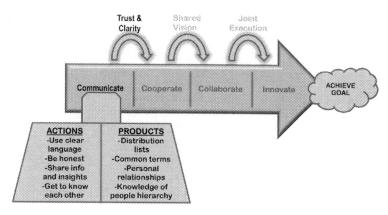

The typical actions from the communication foundation of the IVC should produce trust and clarity among constituents.

While improved behavior is a critical factor, there are tangible products such as distribution lists, common terminology, personal relationships, and so on that reflect how well a group of individuals have bonded.

> **"The void created by the failure to communicate is soon filled with poison, drivel, and misrepresentation."**
>
> —C. Northcote Parkinson

Cooperate

During the next phase of the IVC, the community leverages the trust and clarity developed in the communication phase to focus on listening and sharing. The *American Heritage Dictionary* defines cooperation as "an association of persons for mutual benefit." The result of this phase is a shared vision that reinforces accountability between individuals' actions, team dynamics, and organizational goals.

The "cooperate" figure lays out some simple business tasks that are considered cooperative actions. These should be emphasized early in the discussion of an organization's activity and with a focus on acting, not just meeting and talking.

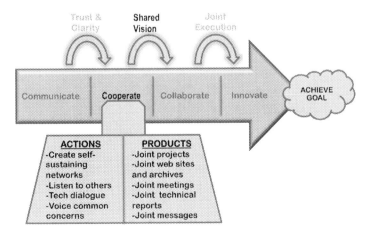

The shared vision expected to form by the end of the cooperation phase should include technical, programmatic, or operational aspects.

Real cooperation takes time and effort. While "active listening" sounds contradictory, the ability to focus on other peoples' needs and wants (over our own) and incorporate them into a shared approach to a problem does take energy and finesse. Cooperation is not simply the lack of arguing but rather the preparatory efforts needed for individuals across diverse organizations to collaborate in positive ways.

Collaborate

The primary action during the collaboration phase of the IVC is to adjust schedules and resource expenditures based upon the joint activities with others. The relationships between parties should have advanced beyond mere access to shared information stores (websites, trip reports, etc.) to cost-share and time-allocation arrangements.

This stage may leverage messaging, repository, and discovery tools and applications to empower learning. Advanced web technologies, such as widgets, wikis, and blogs, may be applied to aid in collaboration. All of these tools contribute to the potential for joint execution that directly leads to our desired end state, innovative results. However, if a group of constituents rushes to have collaborations where messages, insights, data, and products are easily shared among parties without an establishment of trust and a shared vision, increased awareness may just as easily serve to undermine eventual joint execution and success, rather than help it.

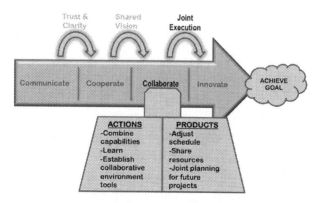

Collaborative activities provide the impetus to execute activities in pursuit of a well-stated and challenging goal, efficiently and effectively.

Specific changes in behavior expected from a successful collaboration phase are the sharing of resources, the adjusting of schedules, and the joint planning of activities. You can tell you are in the collaboration phase by the fact that you allow partner organizations to perform activities critical to your organization. This joint execution is only possible as an offshoot of the trust and shared vision created earlier.

Innovate

Innovation is not necessarily about new items but about creating more valuable results more efficiently (improving outcomes while simultaneously consuming fewer resources). During this last phase, productivity is enhanced, the borders between previously segregated groups are dissolved, and organizational performance is maximized. These benefits do not come easily. They are the result of all the preparatory work done in the previous phases.

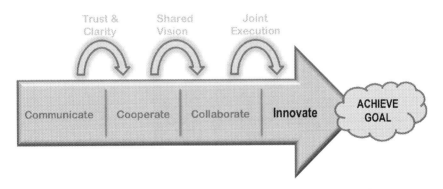

Achieving the goals of a challenging initiative will naturally occur if effort is expended on the phases leading to that point. It will even be difficult to derail success at that point.

The IVC was developed based on observations I made of highly effective teams within SAIC, a $10 billion-per-year defense contractor, and other entities that I have worked with closely over the years. I have applied this to my youth soccer coaching and documented its utility in *Soccer is a Thinking Game* (McKnight, 2009). More recently, the IVC was used to provide an alternative approach for National Space Policy formulation and execution (McKnight, 2011).

The IVC is truly a composite of multiple individual and team innovation tools and principles that are applicable to multiple domains. An outstanding treatise called *Crucial Conversations* that details a comprehensive means to recognize, manage, and succeed in critical discussions in any domain, lays out a framework that parallels the IVC but tailors it to a specific challenge: emotional, important, and immediate dialogues (Patterson, 2002).

Bridgers, Implementers, and Visionaries

In 2005, I was asked to speak at an awards ceremony at the Georgia Institute of Technology. Presenting awards for outstanding papers and celebrating the young, talented authors was exciting but challenging. I was instructed to provide some enduring insight for the graduating engineering and science majors. My message to them was to be true to themselves by realistically ascertaining who they were and then being the best at that.

As a framework for this dialogue, I proposed that there are three major types of people: bridgers, implementers, and visionaries (BIV). Each group is important in its own right. You should not wish to be one of these if you clearly do not have the appropriate skills or interest. While this may seem overly restrictive or constraining at first blush, this exercise is actually, to the contrary, quite liberating.

Coming to grips with which type you are in your firm, your office, or your department, takes some introspection. In addition to knowing what each type of person does, you also need to be aware of the relationships among these prototypical people. This may sound similar to the Myers-Briggs Type Indicator construct, which strives to characterize people by their innate qualities. My BIV framework is much less precise and more focused on job performance related to organizational dynamics rather than on individual personalities related to individual interactions.

Lots of implementers are needed in an organization, many more than either visionaries or bridgers. Implementers are practical and relish filling in the triangles on Gantt charts. They are the ones who do the work on projects and programs but do not necessarily come up with the design for the solutions. They are often specialists in certain fields and are proud of that focus. Sometimes, implementers are junior or mid-level personnel who do not supervise anyone or maybe just other, more junior, implementers.

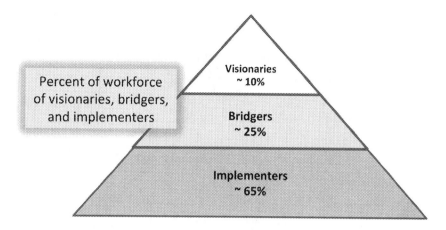

In contrast, there are very few visionaries in an organization in comparison to the implementers. Visionaries are often generalists, or maybe specialists in several areas, but they are usually not very practical. They have the ability to imagine what could be but generally are not be able to actually implement any of their great ideas.

Visionaries are often very seasoned individuals but need not be. They are always creative, with high energy, but usually do not relish managing—or often even dealing with—people. A lyric by the music group Bad Company appropriately sums up the two-edged sword for visionaries: "Geniuses? I'm not in the market for geniuses geniuses tire easily then they brood then they plot."

The last group consists of bridgers. Bridgers are the ones who interface between the visionaries and the implementers. They are pragmatic but also understand the insights of the visionaries. Bridgers enable a final acceptable solution using the positive aspects of both implementers and visionaries. There are a few bridgers in a successful organization, more than the visionaries but many fewer than the implementers. The bridgers provide the fuel for strategy while the implementers are all about tactics. Bridgers may do this joining function in a variety of ways:

- Translating: interpreting insights from implementers and visionaries

- Educating: aiding teaching and learning between other contributors
- Catalyzing: igniting connections between constituents
- Aggregating: amassing components from disparate sources and domains
- Integrating: combining contributions into a coherent design

The key to the success of a company or organization is the mix and mixing of these three types of people. The cognitive diversity of these three groups of people is the key component of the success of an organization, but this diversity has both positive and negative aspects.

Innovation is encouraged by providing a recipe that includes ingredients, constraints that must be followed (e.g., cooking temperature and order of mixing ingredients), and general activities (e.g., coarsely chopping onions). Like any recipe, some people can use it to make a masterpiece, while others may produce a disaster; so there is always room for interpretation and differing levels of competence in execution.

So, does one's DNA destine one to be an implementer, bridger, or visionary? Clearly, there are attributes of these three roles that imply that implementers are the most junior. What else would one be if you have not developed the people skills to act as a viable bridger or the technical clout to be considered a credible visionary? However, there may be prodigies who are so-called old souls and are natural communicators, or brilliant youth who skyrocket to the top of their chosen professions.

There are even rare influential people, such as Bill Gates or Jack Welch, who have served all three roles nearly simultaneously, or at least in rapid succession. Could you have a ten-person firm full of Bill Gates' clones? The answer is not for long!

Even Bill Gates fairly quickly migrated toward being the visionary by hiring the implementers and bridgers to execute. He did prove himself at the implementer and bridger levels and quickly moved on to the visionary position. Bill Gates was an exceptional visionary largely due to the fact that he had earned the respect of his entire organization by having risen through the ranks. Some never move into a visionary position either due to their own choice or their lack of innate abilities.

It is a reasonable hypothesis that the best visionaries did indeed start as implementers but then jumped quickly to the visionary role given the circumstances.

Implementers become bridgers when they start to merge insights from multiple disparate groups (and enjoy it)! When that experienced soldier goes to work for Dell computer and helps them address the operational needs of the warfighter, he has become a bridger. Just communicating between soldiers, maybe as a squad leader, does not make him a bridger.

It is also evident that the role that one takes on is very dependent on the context. Many bridgers appear to be visionaries to some groups and implementers to others, while they know that their primary skills are as bridgers. The bridger's ability is actually dependent on his ability to deal comfortably with both visionaries and implementers, so as a result he must be able to assume the persona (in a positive, nonpejorative manner) of either an implementer or a visionary, at least temporarily. *You might say they need to act as pragmatic visionaries.*

How do you know if you are a good bridger? When I served as the director of science and technology at SAIC, I had to come to grips with that question. We were a corporate office responsible for representing the technical workforce (i.e., implementers) to senior executive management (i.e., visionaries, possibly). This role required us to interface constantly with both camps, yet the standard corporate office staff members are seen as non-revenue-generators by executive management and as bean counters by the rank and file that generate revenue.

To manage this potentially tenuous situation I came up with a metric for my staff that focused on not being an irritant. More specifically, I said that in all conversations with SAIC employees, whether face-to-face or on the phone, we had to strive to keep a very high V-to-E ratio. E referred to the effort that the employee had to put into their conversation with my staff member. This was usually their valuable time, but it might also have been their missing out on another opportunity. The V stood for the value the employee received from the interaction with me or my staff. Clearly, if the V value was zero it would be difficult to have a high V/E ratio! Making this even more difficult was the fact that employees—not me or my staff—defined both the V and the E terms! This forced our folks to really listen and learn what each employee cherished most.

Below is the simple checklist that formed as we planned meetings and phone calls.

- Am I bringing any value to the employee? If not, do not have the meeting, make the call, or send the e-mail. Get the information some other way.
- Am I taking the minimum amount of time for the interaction? If not, figure out ways to minimize the interaction time with the employees.

Our small office was very successful, with the primary metric being that people invited us to meetings (can you imagine inviting corporate to a meeting on purpose?) and returned our phone calls. Being a bridger is rewarding, but bridgers must not forget that they exist to serve the visionaries and implementers.

My hypothesis is that you should strive to be the best at whatever you decide you are or want to be. In doing so, expend energy, be incrementally aggressive, and employ introspective honesty (i.e., do not lie to yourself).

1 = unimportant 10 = critical	Need Practical, Domain-Specific Knowledge	People Skills	Creativity
Visionary	5	2	9
Bridger	6	9	6
Implementer	9	4	2

Being a visionary is great work if you can get it! Most organizations need very few, if any, visionaries. They need to be expert at creative thought, with credible technical knowledge, but may survive with minimal personal skills.

Alternatively, a bridger has the maximum flexibility in continuing and getting work. He or she must listen, learn, and write things down while being a people person. A bridger should have a balance of domain-specific knowledge and creative skills. This is the most difficult combination to achieve or find. In addition, a bridger must be able to quickly acclimate to new situations.

Last, implementers are the most crucial component of a successful organization since there is no value from a group if it cannot execute. For the implementer, domain-specific knowledge is the most important quality, with significant crossover possible with appropriate training. There are many more of these positions available and needed.

This is the perfect final essay, as it hints at the most critical of an innovator's role, that of the pragmatic visionary. The pragmatic visionary is both the glue that holds an organization together and the fuel that can accelerate an organization forward into new, more productive dimensions.

Epilogue

All innovation must be simple, but it is not necessarily easy. Success comes to those who respectfully analyze the past; examine the present through appreciative enquiry; and reach for the future with positive intent and energy. Innovation is systematic creativity since, without process, you cannot hope to repeat successes, but with too much process, you will be doomed to repeat failures.

"Believe in something bigger than yourself."
—Carlos Gutierrez

There are thousands of axioms and observations about innovation. I have tried to narrow these down to dozens of the most useful in this book. However, five innovation principles in particular have served as the core for me in addressing and solving dilemmas over the years. The pillars of innovation are necessarily a cross-section of individual, team, and organization fundamentals. They constitute the closest thing to a cheat sheet for innovation. These approaches have been covered significantly throughout the course of the book.

These are the pillars of innovation:

- Practice and apply superb communications skills.
- Emphasize the high-touch aspects of innovation even as our world becomes more high tech.
- Embrace cognitive diversity when forming teams.
- Execute all activities in small but challenging increments (i.e., act in a way that is incrementally aggressive).
- Apply the Innovation Value Chain (IVC) to the functioning of your organization. The IVC leverages the other four pillars in order to be successful.

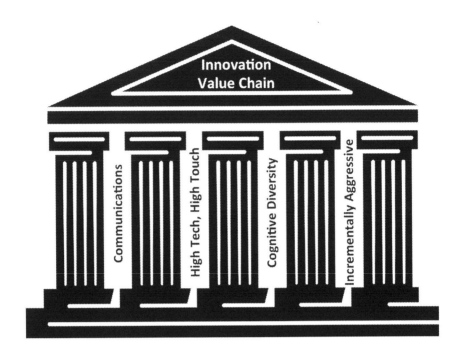

This is not a comprehensive set of principles; but they have served as a coherent suite for me, and I have used every innovation principle described in this book multiple times in my career. You need to examine all of my essays and the guest essays to determine which combination of fundamentals resonate most with you. The collection will change depending upon your challenge and may even change as the problem is "solved," which usually just means that the problem has only evolved into a different, yet still challenging, phase where you may have to apply a different set of fundamental innovative principles. Just as a company evolves from a start-up enterprise into a viable medium-sized company and then an industry-leading behemoth, the techniques to manage the company will also evolve.

No two organizations are the same, so the way in which each empowers and implements innovation will be different. No author or disengaged so-called thought leader can tell you how your organization will optimally apply these basic tenets. It requires that the innovation catalysts of the organization listen carefully, apply appropriate innovation rules and tools, and maintain connectivity between the implementers and the visionaries.

"Nothing is ever achieved without enthusiasm."

—Ralph Waldo Emerson

Michael Gelb, in his 2003 treatise on genius, provided a valuable summary of innovation insights without ever even uttering the word *innovation*. As he so astutely noted, "Wisdom is borne out of the ability to observe and think simultaneously." This wisdom is further developed by listening, questioning, and thinking—anything but talking! The single statement summarizing one of the core essentials of all ageless innovation approaches is this: "Great thinkers listen first" (Gelb, 2003).

During my time as a physics professor, I often told my students that people learned the most right after a brief period of confusion. That is a key to real innovation. Do not be afraid of uncertainty or ambiguity. Understanding that addressing the unknown is usually the point that comes right before someone making a breakthrough should help people work through the normally uncomfortable times that are linked to being challenged by a difficult dilemma or confounding contradiction. I discussed earlier that contradictions often present the greatest opportunities for innovation, so look for dilemmas. In chaos comes opportunity for innovation!

Early in the era of seafaring exploring, captains would navigate with coasts in view since it was thought that the world was flat and sailing away from land would be very risky. However, the *real* explorers did exactly the opposite and headed away from land; they embraced uncertainty and made history. Similarly, modern-day innovation explorers, must be able to head away from the safety of the coast. Be optimistic and treat setbacks as learning experiences. This will enable you to achieve success through innovative breakthroughs. Your future will be bright!

"Simplicity is the ultimate sophistication."

—Leonardo da Vinci

The guest essays that follow are also wonderful examples of how others have applied basic innovation fundamentals in a variety of endeavors that will both amuse and inspire you. In addition, these essays will reinforce the concepts set forth in this book that basic principles of innovation are widely applicable and, when tailored to a specific challenge, can produce amazing results.

Guest Innovation Essays

A fundamental innovation directive presented in this book is to embrace cognitive diversity. I propose that the best way to solve a difficult problem is to get assistance from outside the domain in which you normally reside and where the problem was created. For this reason, I have asked several of my most talented, creative, and professional colleagues to contribute a short essay to this book to provide a more diverse examination of innovation. The guest essayists range from a recent college graduate to a retired civil servant, from the mathematically astute to the musically inclined, from a leader in youth sports to a figure in national politics, and on and on.

I asked them to describe the concepts that have driven their greatest accomplishments and breakthroughs in their professions or to simply wax philosophical about innovation. Despite the wide range of communities covered by these guests essayists, however, the core principles exposed in *Hitting the Innovation Jackpot* are reinforced as common threads in these essays: shared vision, simplicity, communication, value, trust, action, being incrementally aggressive, and cognitive diversity. This not only reinforces the thesis of the book but provides examples of how these repeatable processes have been tailored to bring different organizations value.

The Value of Performance

Eric D. Garvin, Global Hawk manager,
Northrop Grumman Corporation

Successful companies realize that embracing the laws of innovation drives success in very competitive marketplaces. For three decades, I have served in the defense industry, including twenty-six years as an officer in the United States Air Force. During those twenty-six years, I worked mainly on the F-22 Raptor and CV-22 Osprey programs. Over the past four years, I have served as the Washington, DC, manager for the RQ-4 Global Hawk, an air force system adopted by the US Navy, which has become a multibillion-dollar flagship program for Northrop Grumman Corporation (NGC). My experiences in the USAF, in the defense industry, and at the United States Air Force Academy have shaped my views on innovation.

As cadets at the United States Air Force Academy, Darren McKnight and I learned some of the most important laws of innovation, yet we did not think of them as innovation at the time. We both served in Fighting Fourth Squadron, which won an unprecedented three consecutive Honor Squadron Awards during our tenure. The Honor Squadron Award is the most prestigious group award at the Academy, since it honors the top squadron from a field of forty squadrons for academic, athletic, and military performance. Today, Apple and Google are the envy of the business world. In the late 1970s and early 1980s, Fighting Fourth Squadron was the envy of the entire cadet wing at the Air Force Academy.

Many at the Academy often asked, "What is the secret of Fourth Squadron's success?" We had a vision to be the best, and the more than one hundred members of our squadron shared that vision. We worked as a team, with collaboration as our standard mode of operation. Fourth Squadron had such a diversity of talent: some were athletes, some were scholars, some were visionaries, some were bridgers, while others were the foot soldiers. We had a few rare individuals—Dr. Darren McKnight, Marvin Fisher, Major General Tom Masiello, Dr. Jeff Anderson, Dr. Sean Murphy, and Dr. Dean Carlson, to name a few (with their current designations)—who served in all of the roles above.

Simply put, Fighting Fourth Squadron had extraordinary success because we put the laws of innovation into practice by acting on them. We defined, communicated, and embraced a shared vision based on achieving a simple yet ambitious objective. John C. Maxwell, a noted leadership expert, writes, "One of the most valuable benefits of a vision is that it acts like a magnet by attracting, challenging, and uniting people." Second, we worked as a team by embracing our cognitive diversity as a strength. Above all, we executed to deliver exceptional performance.

One of the ultimate objectives of innovation is to derive value. NGC's latest branding campaign is "The Value of Performance." As we perform on our defense contracts, we inherently provide value to our Warfighter customers, while simultaneously providing value to NGC. When we provide value to the Warfighter, it creates a chain reaction. Providing value drives business growth, helps to increase profits, helps to preserve market leadership, and strengthens our financial position to enable us to invest in innovative ideas. By constantly and consistently reinventing products in the defense industry, companies keep their products relevant to the Warfighter, helping to ensure persistent demand.

It is important we do much more than reinvent products; it is imperative to adopt a business culture that promotes the development of products that are rapid, agile, and cost effective (RACE). This is particularly true of the defense industry. Companies that want to survive and thrive no longer have the luxury of being reactive. We must lead with innovative ideas. Simply put, we must define the future, not merely shape it.

At the Air Force Academy, I had the opportunity to be part of an innovation experiment in which one hundred focused professionals executed at the highest levels for three years. Now I have the privilege to help shape how eighty-five thousand dedicated NGC employees can create value for our nation for years to come.

Keep Technical Content Simple, Team Skills Diverse, Goals Focused, and Learn

Donald J. Kessler, NASA senior scientist (retired), Orbital Debris Research

I have been described as one of the key individuals who shaped the programs currently concerned with debris in Earth orbit. Over a twenty-year period, I participated in building these programs as they grew from being nonexistent to being international programs. Sixteen years after my retirement from NASA, these programs continue to expand. I am frequently asked how I got interested in orbital debris. The simple answer would be curiosity; however, without a basic set of mathematical tools, an understanding of customer needs, and a team with diverse organizational skills, no one would be asking me that question today because my curiosity would have led nowhere.

I wasn't the first to think that orbital debris could be a problem. In the late 1960s to early 1970s, others looked at the growing number of large objects in Earth orbit with concern, but they missed the fundamental problem because they incorrectly assumed that the only hazard came from objects large enough to be seen from the ground with telescopes and radars.

These early investigators were using their familiar mathematical tools, such as equations, that had been developed to calculate the orbital positions of objects that were large enough to be tracked by radar. Even if they had accepted the possibility of a much larger debris population (that is, larger than what they could see from the ground), they did not have the tools to adequately address the dynamics.

Not having the right tools for the job increases the difficulty of solving a problem. I consider my primary tools to be the mathematical equations necessary to build models, relate physical parameters to other physical parameters, and predict consequences. These tools are as necessary to a theoretician as a telescope is to an astronomer or a scalpel is to a surgeon. I had the advantage of a being trained in a different organization, one that treated collision frequencies statistically rather than deterministically. However, some of the mathematical tools relating orbits to collision frequency were still overly complex, so I took a fresh approach. This breakthrough was possible only because I transferred tools from one domain into another domain (I thought outside the box). Out of this approach emerged a rule of thumb that I've found useful: *When solving a complex problem, make the simplest assumption first; it may not give you the right answer, but at least you'll know what the answer means.*

While others developed complex geometric equations to relate orbits directly to collision frequency, I broke the problem down into components that were easier for me to understand and were useful for other applications. Each component could then be examined independently. As a result, I was able to derive a general set of mathematical tools that could be expressed in terms of either exact or approximate solutions involving averages.

Mathematical tools with these characteristics easily lend themselves to another important rule of thumb that focuses on simplicity of execution: *If you cannot find an approximate solution to a problem on the back of an envelope, then you do not know what you are doing.*

Back-of-the-envelope solutions not only provide important insight into other variables but are also important reasonableness-checking tools for more exact solutions. Without them, one may never recognize a simple coding error in elaborate computer-driven solutions. In addition, if one fully understands the limitations of any assumption in a back-of-the-envelope solution, one can more easily recognize either what may need to be done differently or how to further build upon that assumption. This learn-as-you-go approach to problem solving facilitates collaboration among fellow scientists of varying backgrounds.

As a responsible researcher, I published my results in a professional journal, and that publication caught the attention of the press. I really did focus early on listening, learning, and writing things down, as this was a brand-new field of aerospace engineering. The resulting publicity of my papers raised both public and NASA management awareness of the issue. As a result, my supervisors opened doors to levels of the organization that were not accessible to me previously. Garnering this type of management support was essential for the program to develop: *With management as a partner, providing the needed resources and establishing connections at higher management levels, one individual can make innovative breakthroughs.*

In a healthy manager-employee relationship, the manager works for the employee in many of the same ways that the employee works for the manager. Through networking outside the organization, the possibilities of new resources, new approaches, and strong coalitions may be found that become essential to the program. *Networking outside your own organization contributes to building a strong team.*

Networking through both formal and informal contacts, describing the program to others, listening to their interests, and looking for opportunities to satisfy their needs and interests while advancing the program's needs are critical to building an effective team.

After a few years of building the case for an orbital debris program, the program was approved by NASA. Some of the individuals from the broad network that had been established joined the NASA program; others supported it from the outside, later becoming part of national and international organizations that they helped to develop. From such a network grew a diverse team of researchers in various organizations, all with a common goal.

Coordination with commercial industries and other government agencies expanded the program nationally. The program naturally grew into a successful international organization as a result of the insightful actions and cooperation of similarly focused individuals within a growing network. The current NASA cadre, who have built upon what I started, is addressing a growing space hazard in orbital debris and their eventual effectiveness will affect all space missions in the years to come.

How to Keep Process Standards from Hindering Innovation
Bob Mitchell, corporate strategist and partner, CIO Partner, Inc.

I have more than twenty years of IT and strategy leadership experience, with direct involvement in corporate strategy and process improvement; product line and program management; software development; and infrastructure management. My education at the University of Texas at Austin (a bachelor's degree in computer science and a master's in business administration) established a strong technical foundation, which I have frequently leveraged to apply innovative concepts in my industry.

Process standards such as those of the International Standards Organization (ISO) and the Capability Maturity Model (CMM) have had very positive impacts on many companies. Customers often require companies to be certified in these standards before they will consider doing business with them. I believe, however, that the nature of those potential process impacts is often misunderstood by executives and key leaders in organizations, especially with regard to process improvement and innovation. For innovation in particular, it appears that many people, even successful executives, believe that innovation is basically a mysterious process only understood by a few people with a unique perspective. Implied in that view is the belief that innovation is a long shot and thus, for most companies, is a major risk that will cost money. As a result, many look for *less* innovation, often through formal process improvement programs that leverage industry process standards.

It may seem strange, then, that these same programs intended to support innovation, actually kill innovation in many companies. Some of these programs yield good results, but I have seen a majority of these programs create little improvement while creating a new layer of bureaucratic overhead. This usually leads to resentment and complacency from many of the middle managers.

I have seen numerous sponsoring executives who don't understand the benefits and liabilities of pursuing an ISO or CMM certification. For example, these programs determine only if you have written down what you do and how you do it, along with verification of each. Value is not a natural byproduct of these actions. The only improvement created in these programs is that a foundation is created for common terminology; process consistency and adherence; and, hopefully, a feedback mechanism for resolution of process failures. These are valuable to many organizations, but most expect that there will be much more value accrued from these onerous processes than merely facilitating enhanced communication and cooperation. As a matter of fact, there are much more efficient ways to garner those benefits—well short of completing an ISO or CMM certification.

Further, process standards do not recommend cost-effective staffing, automation, or removal of process steps. They simply improve the odds that you do what you say you do, good or bad. Relying on a certification to generate process improvement can also create a crutch for managers in the organization, giving the perception of value generation. In top companies, executives thoroughly understand not only their customer expectations and financial objectives but also their core processes, and they are engaged at all levels to create employee ownership and an expectation of improvement.

Ideas are generated at all levels of the organization. Executives must stay engaged to make sure that appropriate projects are selected; key objectives are understood; all relevant personnel are involved and accountable; and resistance to change is addressed. The bottom line is that most corporate innovation is carried out in a disciplined manner that is complementary to formal standardization programs—but not the result of ISO and CMM certifications.

Attention to Detail

Chris Haddock, head football coach, Centreville High School, Virginia

I have the best job in America! I am a high school football coach. I have found over the last nineteen years that coaching football is the next best thing to playing football. As my body will no longer allow me to play, I have to let my mind take over instead. After coaching and playing many sports, I have come to the conclusion that football is the ultimate team sport. In baseball, a pitcher can dominate and often single-handedly win games. In basketball, a point guard can take over a game.

In football, though, a great running back needs help from his line to protect him. A prolific quarterback needs that line as well but he also needs receivers to catch his passes. An offense can run away from a great defender and not let him control a game. Unless there is a complete team, there cannot be consistent success at a high level in football. Even having solid players at every position is often not enough. There needs to be a unifying force that binds these players together to make them a team and not just a group of players.

The players on my team are from the surrounding community adjacent to Centreville High School in the suburbs of Washington, DC. Many have grown up together and now are going to high school together. Most of these student-athletes have varying family dynamics, cultures, religions, socio-economic statuses, ages, grade point averages, and personalities. Not to mention each player is different in physical size, strength, and ability level. There are so many factors that go into the makeup of a team. The challenge for me and my staff is to bring these differences together to form a cohesive unit that can be successful at a high level.

As the head coach, it is my job to oversee the entire program and make sure that my staff and team are executing to a single set of goals, philosophies, and beliefs. The coordination and integration of these commonalities with the diversity of my player population is the critical first key to success and is also, I believe, where the innovation lies. There needs to be a shared, understandable, and memorable theme that *all* of my staff and players can rally around.

This unifying force is our uncompromising belief in attention to detail. There certainly are many details to attend to, and an outsider may observe them to be minutiae that borders on overkill. Our staff believes that our attention to detail and our insistence that our players follow that maxim will develop skill sets that will in turn reward them with victories on and off the gridiron. We contend that players will develop discipline, organization, leadership, consistency, focus, concentration, and a sense of responsibility through their attention to detail. These characteristics will not only help them to be successful on a football field but also with their lives beyond the game. The reality is that most of my players will not be professional athletes, but they will need an array of qualities to help them succeed in whatever endeavors they pursue. The foundation for these characteristics is attention to detail.

Each player, no matter who he is, can successfully follow our instructions and be measured equally to his peers. I have many players who can't catch or throw a ball. I have many players who aren't fast and cannot tackle well. The focus on personal action and responsibility over performance makes our march to success an incrementally aggressive process that cannot fail since our measure of success is commitment and that depends only on our individual and collective actions and not the result of football games.

The details that you choose to insist upon in any given field can be your own, but they need to be selected at a level that can be achieved by everyone. These are some of the details we insist upon: Our helmets are always on and *buckled* until permission is given to remove them. We *never* lean over or on teammates after a sprint or play. Our heads are *always* up on our offensive preset position. When we are in the huddle, we *always* have our *right* hands holding our *left* wrists behind our backs. We *always* run on and off the field unless there is an injury. When I address the team, I expect *all* eyes on me at *all* times.

These are just a few examples of some of details we require within a given day. There are many more, but the point is that these details are basically non-football-related in nature. They are designed to be simple and easy to successfully complete by everyone every single time. To me that is true discipline. Discipline is not attained through punitive measures but by requiring simple, even mundane, tasks to be done correctly *every* time. Once my players internalize that ideal and make it habitual, we can add more tasks and responsibilities to their daily regimen. We also use this model with the teaching of technique and fundamental training. We start with simple steps and add more details as we go. I ask my players regularly, "If you can't hold the correct hand in the huddle or take a step with the proper foot, how can the coaches expect you to make an important play in a crucial situation when the stadium is filled and the pressure is on?"

The consistent pursuit of attending to details is tedious. It requires constant attention and continual reinforcement, especially in the early stages. However, over time, the players will start to demand detail orientation of themselves and their peers. This leadership and level of responsibility is paramount. Again, the players are not demanding football success from each other. They are asking for the completion of many small tasks, and there is no player who can argue that he cannot complete them. That is the inherent innovation of the entire model. *All* can succeed and contribute to the cause. When you are guaranteed productivity at the base level, you are quicker to get buy in to the theme or the goal. The success is constant and can be built upon daily, which deepens the devotion to the way it is achieved.

To me, the premise is simple, and the results are observable. Demanding attention to detail allows lesser players to achieve and contribute, and it makes already good players better. In a high school setting where the players are not recruited or chosen, I need every young man to give me his best and play at the highest level possible. When every player is doing that, special seasons can be had and championships won. I can only imagine, if similar techniques were applied in the workplace, how shared vision, incremental aggressiveness, and action-oriented execution could empower greater workforce productivity.

[Author's Note: In Coach Haddock's first year as head coach in 2010, he turned his program around from a 3-7 record in 2009 to a 9-3 record. In 2011, his team is undefeated and heading to the playoffs as this book goes to print.]

Innovation Starts with Listening

Radovan Pletka, soccer trainer

I have played soccer my entire life and have been a soccer trainer for my entire adult life. Starting during my teenage years in Ghana and through my competitive soccer career in the United States and Europe, I always focused on playing the game but never really had a real plan of execution. However, I remember my first coach scratching out plays in the dusty, grassless fields in Ghana; I loved those early years with my refugee Liberian coach. As I got better and progressed through my high school, college, and professional career, nothing distracted me from my focus on getting the ball into the net!

After my professional career was cut short due to injuries, I settled into a soccer trainer job in northern Virginia. There I enjoyed coaching youth soccer, following traditional training approaches until a fateful hot August day in Chantilly, Virginia. I had been hired to help with a girls' soccer team during a summer camp on a busy, plush grass field. Halfway through the practice, I saw the girls gathering around their coach as he discussed something with them. He gave the girls sheets of paper with diagrams; the girls would scribble on their sheets, and then they would all get back together again.

As the girls went off to do some conditioning training, I spoke to the coach, and he explained that he had a series of written "Chalk Talk" lessons for key aspects of soccer that described game situations in a visual, interactive way for these nine-year-old girls. He stated confidently that this was how they learned math, English, science, and history, so why not soccer? I thought back to my coach scratching out plays in the Ghanaian dirt and made an incredible link: kids learn better using visual, interactive lessons rather than the methodical, rote repetition on the field that I had become so accustomed to over the years.

Through our conversation, I discovered that this coach didn't know much about the game of soccer. He was just a parent coach and career scientist who looked at soccer completely differently than any other coach I had ever met. He was actually applying techniques he used to teach his college physics students to young girls on the soccer field. What I have now come to understand, which he already knew, was that visual thinking (thinking with pictures) can help youth athletes remember details of both simple and complex situations. The most amazing thing is that this team, coached by the professor-engineer who could barely spell soccer, performed well—and in many cases, better than most of the teams in their division and age group.

With further research, I discovered that former NFL coach and team owner Paul Brown, considered the father of the modern offense and one of the greatest football coaches in history, introduced numerous innovative coaching methods still in use today. Mr. Brown was actually the first coach to use classroom techniques to *teach* his football players.

The cognitively diverse team formed by me (the avid, experienced soccer player from Africa) and this scientist-teacher from Virginia came together from that day forward. I subsequently coauthored *Soccer is a Thinking Game* with this coach, Darren McKnight, a book that combined my years of soccer experience with his innovative communication techniques to create a truly revolutionary new approach to coaching youth soccer. The way that I train kids, from six-year-olds to high school varsity players, has changed due to this chance encounter. I have noticed that my teams are definitely playing smarter and are much more aware about what they are doing on the field. In addition, the parents of my players are more informed and, therefore, more supportive of my coaching.

Darren and I both benefited from this enduring relationship because we were both willing to learn something from each other. As Dr. McKnight explains in *Hitting the Innovation Jackpot,* innovation is only possible if you start with a strong foundation of communication and listen with positive intent. Before my encounter with Darren, I used to hate going to soccer clinics and coaching courses because I always thought I knew all that I needed to know about soccer. However, I began to understand that it isn't necessarily about the class itself, but what you can learn from the other attendees, regardless of their qualifications. I am a better coach now, and my teams and players are benefiting simply because I was willing to learn from a refugee from Liberia, a scientist in America, and an iconic football coach.

Never Practice, Always Perform

Sterling Crew, musical artist, technologist, and producer, theENTANgIBLES

"Never practice, always perform." I heard that somewhere once, and it brought me back to the days of remembering to "feel it"—and not "think it"—when I was performing live. In retrospect, that was a giant leap I didn't know I had to face in my early years in the music industry.

Carlos Santana was the teacher, and I was the twenty-six-year-old student. The only problem was that class was held in front of ten thousand to eighty thousand people for every show. I had just joined the Santana band, as a keyboard and synthesizer player, and was basically thrown into the fire on our first tour. Call it tough love, innovative wisdom, or just mimicking one of his mentors, Miles Davis, but Carlos would change the set list every night.

By the end of the first week I had taken notes for all of the thirty-plus songs I had to learn. We rehearsed the following week and then flew off to New York for our first gig the third week. Out of nowhere, twenty minutes before we were about to go on, the stage manager delivered to me major changes in our song list for the evening's concert! And he delivered a cryptic but meaningful message. He looked at me and said, "Carlos said to just play from your heart." The first time this happened, the set list had eight songs taken out and eight new songs put in, six of which I had never heard of. So, I was supposed to just play from my heart, surrounded by tech manuals and my notes as well? This same sequence continued for ten shows, and I was literally exhausted trying to keep up with this phenomenal band of virtuosos, from Carlos' amazing soaring solos, to the steady professionalism of keyboard legend Chester Thompson, and the emotional creativity of percussionist Armando Peraza's real-time brilliance *every night*.

Finally, I realized it was time for a new approach. I picked out my favorite twelve go-to sounds that I knew Carlos liked, and said in my head, "Throw it at me—I'm ready." That's when I started playing from my heart. Of course, then he really threw it at me, but I now had the pleasure of starting to enjoy the shows and responding to the audience, dancing with them, and feeling their energy. I even had my piano modified so I could stand for the whole show. Only then did I finally perform at my highest level, which I would have never attained had I not taken control of the situation.

Are you working on your profession in such a deliberate, consistent fashion? Is this dynamic the same for innovation, or is this only the definition of performance? Is "never practice, always perform" just as applicable to any type of innovation as it is to musical performance?

I think that many professionals such as engineers and scientists are just afraid to say that they "perform." Performing means that you give it your all, so challenge yourself whenever you perform your sport or profession. Musicians know that they are entertainers, and other professionals who want to be the best at what they do should take a little lesson from us. Stop just going through the motions. You need to add passion and enthusiasm to traditional skill in order to create truly new, value-added solutions. To conclude, as a longtime Frank Zappa band member once said, "If your brain has to tell your hands what to play, your fingers are merely wiggling!"

When Innovation Is a Life or Death Proposition

Randy K. Sayles, special agent, deputy assistant administrator (retired), Drug Enforcement Administration (DEA)

In law enforcement, innovation is often a life or death proposition, so we must scrutinize the fundamentals even more closely than other communities. If, when under pressure, engineers do not listen to their peers in order to assimilate a new technique, the project may not perform as well as it possibly could. In dealing with drug interdiction missions and investigations on foreign soil, however, the inability to leverage all information and resources fully may result in complete mission failure or even loss of life.

Law enforcement successes are often directly proportional to leadership's ability to ensure safety during the execution of split-second life and death situations. An exceptional law enforcement leader is usually one with the ability to plan, inspire, and enable appropriate execution in the office and field. This normally requires varied developmental experiences over a period of time in both office and field assignments. Simplicity of mission design, team communications, and organizational reporting drive superior performance since individuals spends their time executing rather than trying to figure out if they are doing the right thing. Clarity is the calling card for joint execution, and the leader must be the advocate for the Agents in the field!

The successful team leader will display exceptional listening skills and an ability to quickly discern between usable and nonusable information. Once this relevant information is assimilated, the team leader will have to communicate the right amount of information to each Agent, as needed. The leader is aware that communication supports cooperation and then collaboration, which eventually leads to innovation. Innovation means that Agents who are in the field in dynamic situations have the knowledge and confidence to execute creatively in order to satisfy their missions while staying within the legal and cultural norms for the situation. This execution is enabled by hours of deliberate practice examining the potential range of alternatives that might manifest themselves in the field.

These activities must focus on communicating details across the full spectrum of law enforcement and intelligence-gathering activities. Many of these are challenges that are not neatly defined according to textbook theories or standard training. The collaborative communication skills of leaders, managers, administrators, and Agents are prerequisites for managing and exploiting the cognitive diversity of these complex teams. We are by definition an organization of diversely skilled individuals that executes optimally when we focus on strong communication techniques.

When multiple agencies have to work together, which is often, not appreciating the importance of cognitive diversity to innovation is debilitating. In addition, two aspects of the sprawling law enforcement infrastructure are often ignored: administrative experts and local contacts in remote sites. In both cases, these experts are lifelines needed for the Agents to succeed. Administrative personnel are capable of helping Agents navigate and use the organization efficiently. The quick processing of travels requests is as critical to mission success as having the correct surveillance tools, but is not always as appreciated. Similarly, the local expert can provide the critical contextual and cultural information about locations for missions that will make or break the operation. Whether or not the local cafes normally cater to foreigners may be the small yet critical feature that will give your team that extra level of protection or insight to ensure mission success.

Quality law enforcement agencies really do live by the maxim that "success comes to those who respectfully analyze the past, examine the present through appreciative enquiry, and reach for the future with positive intent and energy."

Innovation as Pursuit of Happiness?

Michael Overturf, industrial productivity expert and CEO, Nadan Energy,

Innovation is not a new thing. In 1311, some seven hundred years ago, in a three-part writing titled *De Monarchia*, Dante Alighieri feared being dull and unoriginal, wishing his contemplations "to bear fruit by establishing truths unattempted by other." Failing to do so, he mused, "[such] tedious superfluousness would merely occasion disgust" (Alighieri, 1904).

The reader will sympathize with my trepidation at having been invited to write this guest innovation essay. Considering that one of the great minds of the fourteenth century had already worried about being redundant, coupled with the additional hundreds or thousands of brilliant men and women over the subsequent seven hundred years, I am a bit concerned about contributing something new on the topic of innovation. Since there is little I can contribute to the metaphysics of the phenomenon, I will merely examine its politics, traditionally the refuge of scoundrels.

Dante Alighieri went on to argue, possibly the first such elaboration, that men naturally engage in the pursuit of happiness on earth, and that the monarch has the responsibility to lead them to it (he was relegating the pope's power to the afterlife). It is this very pursuit that creates a fertile ground for novelty in culture, science, and society. In effect, I deduce from his contemplations that, only if one is genuine and rational about one's own pursuit of happiness, can tedium and superfluousness be mostly avoided.

Is innovation an effect of the pursuit of happiness?

It was another 450 years after Alighieri that the right to pursue happiness was written as national code in the American Declaration of Independence, to this day without peer. In a messy process the monarch has become an institutional trinity that still can't make up its mind whether it should lead or get out of the way. The monarch has become the state. But does the state lead us to the pursuit of happiness, and thereby, invention and creativity?

Opinions differ, as you may have surmised. Personally, if a representative of the state were to helpfully suggest an act of requisite novelty from me, I would merely provide them with what they asked for, hardly an act of synthesis. On the other hand, it is much more difficult, but not impossible, to be creative when you're hungry, mayhem rules the street, or you're suffering from disease.

I say not impossible, though. Blaise Pascal wrote *Thoughts* (*Pensées*), published in 1670 after his death, while dying slowly and painfully from stomach cancer. In section II, he writes of imagination, *"She makes men happy and sad, healthy and sick, rich and poor; she compels reason to believe, doubt, and deny; she blunts the senses, or quickens them; she has her fools and sages; and nothing vexes us more than to see that she fills her devotees with a satisfaction far more full and entire than does reason."* Pascal describes imagination as a deceitful compulsion, and those thusly afflicted as happy and satisfied. It is unreasonable to be happy and satisfied, he says (understandably, considering his condition).

Innovation, imagination, novelty is not a choice. It is in the nature of man. It is a pursuit, an effort. You want to get up early and be where you want to be. It is schooling and failure, even trial and tribulation. Innovation itself is a product of freedom because you have to be free to pursue happiness, but it is deceitful because you are precariously free to be wrong about what makes you happy.

Therein lies the monarch's paradox: in order to lead, innovation cannot have a quality for him, yet it is the quality of the common pursuit that indicates his leadership. Innovation is facilitated by the state's secular leadership in a delicate and difficult balance.

The understanding that reason, knowledge, and freedom will beget innovation is not new in the least. But it is an understanding that each generation must renew, while engaging in a continuous conflict on the nature and balance of the monarch's leadership.

Intelligence Analysis as an Exemplar for Innovation
Alicia Santoliquido, intelligence analyst

Intelligence analysis is a field for innovators. It requires providing structure and context to information from a variety of sources in order to reduce uncertainty for a decision maker. It is also what one of my fellow analysts calls a "people business." As these definitions imply, intelligence analysis shares many of the hallmarks of innovation described in this book. It is accomplished by means of communication and cooperation with people of varying professional backgrounds; depends upon a medley of facts and ideas; challenges the analyst to cross-examine data; and, finally, yields thoughtful input to matters essential to mission success.

An intelligence analyst may be a subject matter expert, but is also often a generalist. In other words, the analyst often specializes in *how* to think about a target subject rather than *what* to think about it. The analyst knows a little about many things and strives to objectively consider and draw meaning from data. It is hard for one person to examine a target from a variety of perspectives, or even to collect a breadth of information about it. Leveraging the cognitive diversity found in a cadre of subject matter experts furthers the effort, and provides an opportunity to employ several techniques associated with innovation.

Since collection is an early part of answering an intelligence question, among the first tools of innovation to which an analyst turns is asking questions and listening to responses. This is especially important when he is not an expert of the subject at hand. A willingness to hear many and diverging viewpoints is always involved. The analyst does not meet with experts in order to tell them what he is thinking; rather, he avoids forming judgments until he has collected responses from and considered the validity of his sources.

During and after collecting information, the analyst studies it. The process is similar to solving a crossword puzzle, as earlier described in this book. Crossword puzzles force a person to consider words and phrases from different angles. Is *run* a verb or noun in this clue? Since the answer I'm thinking of does not fit in this space, do I have the wrong answer or is there an alternate spelling? In the same way that people work through crosswords, an analyst asks himself to name as many implications of his collected information as he can, considers what information he has not uncovered, and asks himself what the absence of certain information could mean. He will separate assumptions from fact (i.e., separate context from content) in order to determine the applicability of the information. An analyst does not accept data at face value until he is familiar with its origin, scope, and context.

Intelligence analysts, like other innovators, take an uncommon approach to debates. When most people try to prove a point during discussions or arguments, their tendency is to put forth the evidence that supports their conclusion. Analysts instead assign more weight to disconfirming evidence. The discipline of truly listening while avoiding any organizational psychological inertia pushing one to interpret data to support some preconceived concept or theory is a hallmark of intelligence analysts that contribute mightily to innovative teams. Pieces of information that do not agree with others are not labeled problems, nor are they ignored. The analyst is supposed to look into the other peoples' boxes (discussed earlier in this book) to see what their contents expose about the target of analysis. In the end, mismatched information may indeed be an outlier, and acknowledging it, while not allowing it to impact analytic judgment, is the innovator's way of disagreeing without being disagreeable. It is the work of a professional who must assimilate knowledge from outside his cognitive box yet maintain the thirty-thousand-foot view that allows him to decide what belongs in the final assessment.

Just as there are always challenges for the innovator to conquer, questions that require analytic rigor continually arise. Since most innovation involves applying existing capabilities or techniques, even to new problems, the intelligence analyst returns to the foundational practices mentioned here. In every case, the analyst carefully seeks understanding of available information to derive forward-looking insights that leads to better decision making.

Freedom of Discovery

Frank Di Pentino, strategist and decision support specialist, Integrity Applications Incorporated (IAI)

Recently, I was asked to be part of a small team setting up a new office within a large government organization. This group was charged with addressing an emergent need that, until then, had only been addressed piecemeal by several other organizations but had not mandated the primary attention of any single entity.

Our initial approach involved three critical steps: first, determine the best course of action to address this burgeoning issue; second, develop the technologies and methods necessary to address the problem; and finally, enable and enact that vision across the various stakeholders and contributing organizations by unifying and coordinating the sporadic efforts already underway.

Within a short timeframe, it became evident that an innovative solution would be necessary to address this challenge. Furthermore, it was also apparent that the complementary and supporting elements across the larger community would need to undergo significant transformation to enact the solution. Innovation, therefore, became the critical ingredient that allowed the office to rapidly address the emerging topic in a timely and effective manner. Innovation had to be manifested across three general areas.

Innovation within the organizational structure
Contrary to most new-office formations, senior leadership allowed the team leads unprecedented flexibility. The group manager was instructed to report directly to government seniors, bypassing much of the reporting structure. The manager was also given permission to handpick his staff, regardless of affiliation or existing contract status. The resulting team had a broad range of expertise and experience (truly a "cognitively diverse" team), yet all were common in their track record of questioning and operating outside of the mainstream bureaucracy. This authority was combined with a flat, informal, and hence adroit team structure.

Innovation on the topic area.

We were then allowed to pick the hardest problems within the domain and given broad authority to engage whomever necessary to address those problems. Symbiotic cross-fertilization occurred naturally between project thrusts through meetings that came to be known as whiteboard sessions. In these gatherings, many of the team members would coalesce to brainstorm new paths on individual efforts, while simultaneously assuring consistency in terminology and action across all of the parallel efforts. Most important, however, was the overarching evaluation climate that gave each of us the permission to fail, while simultaneously being held accountable for the decision process and conclusions. In retrospect, this was the single most significant factor contributing to innovation.

Innovation across the entire value chain.

Once a broad strategy had been established, we were given authority to evangelize that message across the entire community. What we unearthed were two groups of people. The first group shared our vision and had discovered similar opportunities within their particular portion of the value chain, but they were confronted with an organizational structure that presented obstacles to success. The second group thoroughly believed in the stability, consistency, and predictability of the bureaucracy; unfortunately, this second group also erroneously assumed that innovation was designed to supplant, rather than complement, the existing bureaucracy. This autoimmune response forced our group to innovatively operate in a more insurgent-like fashion, in which we were able to form a coalition of the willing that informally instated many recommendations at the individual rather than operational or programmatic level. This was accomplished through working groups, joint papers, and other purposeful reverse propagation responses to a classically linear process (i.e., cross talk between early-stage and late-stage systems). All of these efforts allowed the individual components (the coalition of the willing) to organize and execute cooperatively without having an official mandate to do so, thereby bypassing the bureaucracy's defense mechanism to change.

During our second year of operation, we were asked to establish a group motto. My recommendation happened to be the group favorite and was quickly adopted as our tagline: Freedom of Discovery. I believed then, as I still do today, that this motto succinctly encapsulated the factors that enabled success. However, it should be noted that these innovative factors were necessary, but not sufficient, for success. There was still some mysterious magic sauce that made it all possible. We needed an eclectic mix of individual talents, creativity, timing, organizational inertia, and historic events to facilitate the effective deployment of our innovative tiger team.

As an epilogue, though, I must mention that the project team still faces significant hurdles, which trace back to one key factor. I mentioned that we were given authority to enact and evangelize our mission; however, the group was never granted the final authority to interrupt the bureaucracy (via funding or other putative means) should the existing structure choose to ignore the recommendations of the innovation team. Therefore, I cannot stress enough the importance of full management commitment should an organization truly wish to innovate. As detailed in *Hitting the Innovation Jackpot*, innovative individuals executing under innovative team methodologies can still be derailed if the overarching organization does not support and celebrate innovation.

Innovation as an Antiprecedent

Eric Eugene Garvin, recent law school graduate

Oyez! Oyez! Oyez! The imperative once used by town criers as early as the fifteenth century to garner attention for a proclamation is still recited in today's US Supreme Court. It is just one example of a tradition that pays homage to heritage. Likewise, in the practice of law, courts and counsel frequently refer to what is known as precedent, in order to determine the strategy for a given case. Precedent is the law's way of stating that the manner in which a court or other deciding authority dealt with a case previously is how those authorities will deal with similar facts and cases in the future. Precedent is both necessary and prudent because it serves as a gatekeeper and guidepost that provides for order and a court system that is fair and balanced, at least ideally. However, when it comes to innovation, I view precedent as less of an equitable gatekeeper and more of an enemy at the gates.

Innovation is akin to what is called a case of first impression. A case of first impression is one in which the reviewing court is weighing a novel legal issue or factual scenario. However, cases of first impression are not the rule, they are quite the exception. They allow courts and counsel to explore new lines of rationale that challenge a standing law that is either inadequate or inequitable. Still, courts are hesitant to "legislate from the bench" and constructively create new laws, because that function is more appropriately reserved for legislative bodies.

Outside of the legal arena, society in general is charged with the responsibility to advance itself. Unlike our judiciary and legislative branches, there are no functional partitions that separate the keepers of tradition from the creators of transition. Therefore, in order for society to truly advance, the opposite of what takes place in a court room or law office must occur in a board room or laboratory, which is to say that innovation and transition must triumph over tradition and precedent.

Whether you are an adherent of creationism or evolution, you can probably agree that intelligent life finds ways to advance, thrive, and provide a foundation for the next generation to do so. Salmon swimming upstream against currents (and conventional wisdom) to spawn are a great example. Within appellate law, once a case can no longer be advanced or appealed to a higher authority, it is appropriate to say the client's appeals have been "exhausted." Without some kind of innovative injection, such as an executive pardon or new evidence leading to exoneration, the client's fate is sealed, and the sentence must be served. I believe a similar analogy applies to those who are not inspired to innovate every day. Similar to prisoners, they are mentally confined to repetitive thought processes and lives of tedium, unless and until they break or are set free.

I believe that innovation glances at the past, but more importantly looks beyond it—and even beyond the present—for the sake of an improved tomorrow. The Wright brothers are a good example of having to glance at the past in order to grasp the future. To be sure, they were acquainted with the reality of physics and gravitational forces. Yet, they took the forces for what they were and challenged them nevertheless. What's more impressive is that the Wright brothers succeeded in innovating by first exposing the shortcomings of tradition (i.e., precedent).

NASA mentions that in order to predict lift and drag, the Wrights used mathematical formulas. At the time of their experimentation, they relied on a value known as the Smeaton coefficient. The Smeaton coefficient had been in use for over a century, but as the Wrights progressed, they began to use different mathematical values, which allowed them to see that the traditional Smeaton coefficient calculations were incomplete at best and possibly even incorrect.

By challenging the traditional values of the Smeaton coefficient, the Wrights will forever be remembered as innovators and the fathers of flight. The case of the Wrights demonstrates that tradition may never disappear and may even have to be wrestled with the entire time that you are attempting to innovate. Unfortunately, in the workplace, we often become smitten with the Smeaton coefficients of life. We are too prone to following the ways that others validate, but that does not produce breakthroughs or innovative results. In too many cases, stubborn adherence to tradition is a hindrance to great innovations taking flight.

Innovation by Acronym

Ken Harvey, retired NFL great; president and CEO, Phezu

Perhaps you know the meaning of the acronym TEAM: together everyone achieves more. Well, while it is true that "together everyone achieves more." I want to share a more comprehensive perspective from my position as a former NFL player and current businessman who sees the parallels between sport and business success every day. This simple axiom has guided many of my successes on and off the field over the years. Let's break TEAM down word by word.

Together

It seems simple enough to do something together, but the sad truth is that we, as a nation and a people, are forgetting what it really means to work together. The Bible talks about *all parts* working together for the good of the whole. In football, we talk about working together on offense, defense, and special teams, but we fail to realize that togetherness means that all of the parts will not look alike. All parts will not and should not be the same, because if they are, this fact will inhibit growth. Togetherness means there is a shared vision that unites the organization to achieve success, however the group defines it.

Everyone

This is important because there is a danger in not including those who are unlike you. We all have skills and talents that can be brought to bear on a problem. If someone has something to offer that could contribute to the organization attaining its objective, we must find a way to leverage these skills. Sometimes we can be so completely like-minded that we lose the ability to shift our perspective. And the very person you reject because of their difference could be the very person who has the missing part needed for your success. For example, in football excluding or minimizing the role of a kicker could mean the loss of those tie-breaking three points.

Achieve

We all have to have a goal or goals to achieve. We have to have a place to go and a way of measuring our progress. The process of achievement is both the place *and* the way we measure success. The effort we put into the game, project, or mission is more important than the result. As players, if we do not try to achieve greatness, then we lose the spirit of competition, that competitive edge that prepares us for a potential win. The greatest challenge is not simply in winning games but rather in *how* we play.

All of those statistics and variables recorded for a player's performance in a succession of games equal that player's overall record of achievement at the end of his career. The same is true in every aspect of life, where measurable outcomes mean the difference between what you should have done and what you actually did or did not do. It is the difference between where you are and where you can go. By being incrementally aggressive and trying to achieve your best every play, every meeting, and every project, you have a much greater chance of attaining greatness over a career.

More

Our country is founded on the principle of hard work. If you work hard enough, you can achieve *more*. When I played football, the "more" in my life was about quality of life: money, success, and well-being. Think about what the world would be like if we did not try to achieve more. There would be no huge corporations providing incomes to the people who drive our economy. The game of football would be pointless and boring as a mode of entertainment if everyone involved, from the owners to the players, was merely content with showing up for the sake of showing up. Most likely, there would be no fans.

Let me point out that there is a fine line between seeking more and being greedy. I consider greed to be "uncontrolled more." Greed generally has no checkpoints or boundaries; it is the pursuit of more without consideration for the team and fans. Pursuing more in life is not a bad thing. With positive intent, it is a vital and necessary part of life. A healthy desire for more is what drives a baby to stop crawling and begin walking. In sports, we try to gain more points than our opponent. We try to achieve the most victories so that we can become winners, but within the framework of more, we still need to act with integrity.

Political, Bureaucratic, and Leadership Elements of Innovation

Paul Byron Pattak, political and business strategist

Since coming to Washington, DC, when I was eighteen, I have spent my entire adult life observing, learning about, and participating in the challenges of facilitating innovation in many fields of endeavor, either on my own account or working in partnership with others. Of the many factors necessary for innovation, my focus today is on political, bureaucratic, and leadership influences.

Innovation can, and does, happen within environments not conducive to its development, just as plants, trees and crops can grow in parts of the world with poor soil and inadequate water. However, that is not a good way to achieve maximum potential. At a time when we need innovation and its fruits more than ever, our challenge is to create those better environments— gardens, if you will—that allow innovation to flourish. We must encourage extraordinary innovation commensurate with the extraordinary challenges we face.

Metaphorically, for innovation to take root and grow, it must be protected; it must be watered; it must be kept from choking; and its seeds must fall upon good soil.

The difference between a bad environment and a good one can be vividly illustrated by a movie reference many of us remember. When my wife and I went to the Island of Kauai for our second anniversary, we visited Allerton Garden, one of the sites where *Jurassic Park* was filmed. During the scene in which the granddaughter of the park's creator gets sneezed on by a brachiosaurus, she is sitting in a tree called a Moreton Bay fig, which is native to Queensland, Australia. We learned that day, that the tree struggles to grow in the dry, arid parts of Australia and can be scrawny. However, when it is planted in the rich volcanic soil of Kauai, doused in one of the wettest climates in the world, and protected from natural predators, it grows to massive proportions.

This botanical analogy maps nicely against politics, bureaucracy, and leadership, and the failings we need to change in each area of influence are fairly straightforward and well within our power, should we muster the will to take them on. While this essay directly addresses what is going on in Washington, DC, the general principles apply to all levels of government or any sprawling organization.

In the realm of politics, sane people need to step in and stop the steadily increasing level of silliness in both political discourse and in political decisions. One of the hallmarks of our success as a country has been that we have treated people, ideas, and capital better than anywhere else in the world. When we question the basis of scientific facts on emotional grounds and cut budgets for programs whose job it is to grow the seed corn for the future, we are damaging ourselves while the rest of the world moves on.

In the realm of bureaucracy, we continue to rely on too many institutions designed during the eighteenth century to solve twenty-first-century problems. We require organizational structures and operating constructs that can move at the speed of the challenges we face. Bureaucracies don't come up with better ways to counter improvised explosive devices (IEDs) in the field; agile and nimble teams do. We also too often uphold the status quo of trapping good people inside bad organizations, and then we wonder why things do not work as well as we would like. There is a place for traditional bureaucracies in the performance of routine function; but a traditional bureaucracy is not where innovation can flourish, and the federal government needs a lot of innovation to take on more complex projects in an era of declining resources. Since they are often not self-sustaining, the success of innovative endeavors such as Lockheed's Skunk Works and similar organizations depends on a larger ecosystem to provide services, resources, and insulation from day-to-day distractions. This in turn allows the team to spend more time concentrating on the problems at hand. Traditional bureaucracy has survived since the time of the pharaohs in Egypt and is not going away soon. *It is the traditional bureaucracy that provides the watering described earlier as a critical element of life support.*

In the realm of leadership, we need to actually start doing more to encourage and nurture innovation. Individuals in leadership positions can choose how they approach their jobs, and history is full of examples in which literally one person made a difference. At Lockheed, Kelly Johnson ran Skunk Works and designed aircraft in record time—often exceeding performance specifications.

The Supermarine Spitfire, the plane known for winning the Battle of Britain, was a radical design that broke with all the known rules and doctrine of aviation at the time. The engineers at Supermarine did all the technical innovation, but it required Air Commodore Henry Cave-Browne-Cave to approve the acquisition of one prototype outside of normal channels for the amount of £10,000 that allowed the innovation to migrate from the workbench to the skies over Britain. *A critical part of leadership is ensuring that neither innovation, nor the innovator, is choked by either bureaucracy or circumstances.*

As a country, we can make this work and create a better garden for innovation. Politics, bureaucracy, and leadership all center around the actions of people, and people can choose to change the world for the better. The good news is that we have done this before and can do so again.

Simple Model Is Simply Successful

Joe Brickey, CEO, Integrity Applications Incorporated

Integrity Applications Incorporated (IAI) is a mid-sized engineering and software services company with a nationwide presence primarily supporting the intelligence community and other civil, defense, and intelligence customers. As chairman of the board and chief executive officer, I am responsible for developing and maintaining a culture that motivates our employees to live our core values. As one of the four founders of this company, I can assure you that we were motivated to build an organization elegant in its simplicity: quality employees in an enlightened organization will produce extraordinary results.

It all starts with trust. A work environment based on trust is a key factor that allows innovation to occur at IAI. In order to foster innovation, you must step back and allow it to happen. Work environments that are based on a rigid command-and-control structure very seldom generate breakthrough ideas and approaches. Trust does not guarantee success, nor will it prevent failure; but it does allow people the freedom to innovate in an environment that is willing to allow experimentation to occur.

IAI has been blessed to assemble a highly motivated workforce and a leadership team that effectively communicates a strong sense of mission, vision, and purpose. It is the leadership team's responsibility to share across the organization the vision and values that helped to create the company in the first place and then to take the time to interact face-to-face with employees to nurture the vision and to execute organization goals. We understand that people innovate and organizations do not! While some organizations attempt to drive innovation using a top-down approach, IAI has found more success through having "Above and Beyond" expectations and allowing innovation to rise up from within the organization. By getting out of the way, leaders can create a work environment where breakthrough discoveries and innovative thinking are possible. Keeping the organizational structure flat and processes non-bureaucratic allows for quick and easy communication between employees and decision makers.

Innovation is not always a well-controlled process. IAI firmly believes that if you bring great people together, great things will happen. You cannot predict in most cases what these great things will be, nor would you necessarily want to do so. IAI leadership facilitates opportunities to bring people together across business areas, functions, and teams, and creates a collegial and open environment where innovation is possible. At IAI, we communicate with employees regularly in a variety of ways, but we have found the greatest success has been in one-on-one encounters or in small group settings.

IAI encourages all employees to bring forward their suggestions and good ideas about how IAI can be made a better place to work, how our products can be improved, and how our service to customers can be enhanced. Individual employees who see an opportunity for improvement are free to discuss it with anyone in IAI leadership, who will then bring the idea to the attention of the people in the company who are responsible for possibly implementing it. Leaders at IAI express appreciation for innovative ideas and regularly champion and implement innovative ideas that employees suggest. No-fault experimentation is encouraged, but results do matter. Rewards are tied to achieving positive outcomes. That said, it is better to have tried and failed than to not have tried at all.

IAI fosters a sense of individual and team ownership for good ideas. People do their best when they are engaged in doing challenging and meaningful work. Individual and collective passion can drive innovation. People take tremendous pride in developing an idea and driving it to implementation. Tapping into individual and team entrepreneurial spirit drives successful organizational outcomes. When an individual or team takes ownership of an idea, they will always put in the additional time, energy, and creativity needed for implementation.

Innovative organizations are entrepreneurial in nature, but each also follows a clear and compelling vision. Going "Above and Beyond" in all things drives IAI to achieve excellence on behalf of our customers. It also is the driving force behind creating and sustaining a work environment where innovation is possible. Our recent selection as the second-best medium-sized workplace in America for the second straight year is a laudable recognition for a simple business model: attract and retain great people and then establish policies to help them succeed.

New and Emerging Ideas about Innovation in Large Organizations

Peter Temes, president, Innovation for Large Organizations (ILO) Institute

In the last twenty years, innovation as a field of applied thought has been dominated by three models: 1) "Lead User" model developed by Eric von Hippel of MIT, 2) "Disruptive Innovation" model championed by Clayton Christensen of Harvard, and 3) "Open Innovation" model developed by Henry Chesbrough of the University of California at Berkeley. Disruptive innovation became the pervasive influence in innovation community thought due to Christensen's influential position at the Harvard Business School, his skill as a presenter, the early backing by Andy Grove at Intel, dedication to outreach, and the well-crafted book *The Innovator's Dilemma*.

Von Hippel's more traditionally academic approach proposed that users of products and systems generally customize them to suit their real-world needs while producers and providers ought to study those modifications in order to learn from them. He brought that powerful idea to the fore and helped companies such as 3M achieve great market gains.

Chesbrough's Open Innovation model has been recognized as a breakthrough idea, highly in sync with the emergence of Internet tools to allow massive collaboration on many business and scientific fronts. Open source software development, collaborative drug discovery, prediction markets, and real-time customer behavior mapping all exemplify core ideas in Chesbrough's model. I will now detail some specifics and implications of Christensen's philosophy on innovation at the organizational level.

Disruption: Clayton Christensen's Innovator's Dilemma

Clayton Christensen's 1997 book *The Innovator's Dilemma* presents some of the most original thinking in the study of business in decades. Looking at two industries, the computer memory hard-drive business (with its rapid cycle of change and high relevance to current industry) and the steam-shovel business (a model of technological change moving slowly enough to allow thorough dissection), Christensen concludes that business innovation comes largely in two types, sustaining innovation and disruptive innovation.

Sustaining innovation is what large, entrenched businesses generally strive to do: 1) take existing products and business models and make them incrementally better over time and 2) introduce new products that dove-tail with existing products, replacing existing products as their value passes optimal points with new products that don't threaten existing franchises.

Disruptive innovation is what insurgent players practice. While sustaining innovation has real value, disruptive innovation has the power to transform industries, and to kill major companies.

Disruptive innovation generally begins with a small player selling a product into an existing market that dominant players view as non-threatening. The new product is usually of lower quality, and solves less ambitious problems than the existing, dominant product solves. Consider the personal computer versus the mainframe. The PC, at the time of its introduction, did not look like a threat to the mainframe, because it lacked the computing power of mainframes. However, the PC secured a niche in the low end of the computing market, established a customer base, developed recognizable market presence, and quickly improved in quality and capacity. Eventually the PC industry squeezed out leading mainframe computer makers like Digital, Wang, and Prime (and decimated IBM's mainframe business, as well).

Again and again, Christensen observed that the fundamental cycle of change that unfolds is that incumbents produce high-cost, high-quality, high-margin goods and services that are displaced by insurgent players offering "good enough quality" on new technology platforms at dramatically lower prices. The insurgents survive off of lower margins but also build new customer eco-systems by, first, serving those priced out of the old marketplace, and then growing to serve the incumbents' best customers, as well. This is the core of the disruptive innovation model: the insurgent wins; the incumbent loses.

Christensen's advice to old-line companies is to practice both sustaining and disruptive innovation by attacking their own existing products with innovative new products on a disciplined, regular basis. As well, they need to look at merger and acquisition as a tool for innovation and to grow business over time by acquiring disruptors. Christensen even told a small group at an ILO Institute meeting that without a doubt, Boeing should have acquired Embrear, the Brazilian manufacturer of regional jets. The regional jets fit the classic model of disruptive innovation as they compete against Boeing's big planes.

A Parallel Development: The new focus on business model innovation
In the past four or five years, innovation advisers of all stripes have been focusing more and more on business model innovation than traditional product and process innovation. Rather than focusing on creating better and more sale-able things and experiences, they have begun to focus on new and different ways of getting paid for what they do. Christensen and his affiliated firm InnoSight have been talking and writing a great deal about "disrupting the business model."

The classic example of business model innovation is the shift in telecommunications services from charging by the minute of service to flat monthly plans. And while many will say that pricing innovation is a subset of business model innovation, my experience working with the member organizations of the ILO Institute is that the only business model innovations that have been truly successful are the pricing-centered examples. Put another way, experience has shown me that business model innovation *is* pricing innovation. And, without a doubt, the most underused tool in pricing innovation is the zero price-point.

Business model innovation has gotten a good deal of focused attention in recent years for three reasons, I believe: 1) The pay-off for successful business model innovation is enormous; 2) We're currently at the end of a multi-year cycle of attention to innovation as a leading business idea, and many of the product- and process-centered models have been tried, with mixed results. Businesses are ready for an emphasis that builds on these recent investments, but also offers something new; and 3) the cost of business model innovation can seem deceptively low. The true cost of business model innovation comes from the fact that it does not always work, and the cost of failure in this category is uniquely high.

With these ideas in mind, the best approach to business model innovation likely builds on Joseph Schumpeter's idea of "creative destruction." Business model innovation will, indeed, empower great change in any organization that proves out a new way of getting paid for what it does. There will be winners and losers, and some of the potential losers will see the future before them and fight it. Plan for the chaos; do not rely on the masters of the old model to lead the new.

References

Alighieri, Dante. *De Monarchia* (English translation). Cambridge: Riverside Press, 1904.

Amabile, Teresa. *The Progress Principle*. Boston: Harvard Business Review Press, 2011.

Anderton, Craig. *"Keeping the 'Art' in 'State of the Art': Are you fighting technology, or flowing with it?"* Last modified February 7, 2011. http://community.jivesoftware.com.

Andrew, James. "Reaping the Rewards of Innovation." *Optimize* (May 2007): 47-48.

Argyris, Chris. "Teaching Smart People to Learn." *Reflections* 4, no. 2 (1991): 4-15.

Beer, M., Eisenstat, R., and Schrader, D. "Why Innovations Sit on the Shelf." *Harvard Business School Working Knowledge Newsletter*, July 26, 2004.

Benton, Steve. "The Wisdom From Within." *Optimize* (October 2006):34-46.

Berkun, Scott. *The Myths of Innovation*. Montreal: O'Reilly, 2007.

Bjoran, K. "Plant a New Language in Your Mind." *MIT Technology Review* (23 June 2011).

Blanding, Michael. "Transforming Manufacturing Waste Into Profit." *Harvard Business School Working Knowledge* (October 3, 2011).

Bossidy, Larry and Charan, Ram. *Execution: the Discipline of Getting Things Done*. New York: Crown Business Books, 2002.

Buderi, Robert. *Engines of Tomorrow*. New York: Simon and Schuster, 2000.

Christensen, C., Kaufman, S., and Shih, W. "Innovation Killers: How Financial Tools Destroy Your Capacity to Do New Things," *Harvard Business Review* (January 2008).

Connolly, Mickey and Rianoshek, Richard. *The Communication Catalyst*. New York: Dearborn Trade Publishing, 2002.

Coyne, K., Clifford, P., and Dye, R. "Breakthrough Thinking from Inside the Box." *Harvard Business Review* (December 2007).

Delong, T.J. and DeLong, S. "Managing Yourself: The Paradox of Excellence." *Harvard Business Review* (June 2011).

Derby, Esther. "Collaboration Skills for Agile Teams." *CrossTalk – The Journal of Defense Software Engineering* (April 2007).

Field, Anne. "Getting a Handle on Employee Motivation." *Harvard Business School Working Knowledge Newsletter* (October 20, 2003).

Gagliardi, Gary. *Sun Tzu's The Art of War for the Management Warrior*. Seattle: Clearbridge Publishing, 2007.

Gallo, Carmine. "Free Webinar: Top 10 Communications Secrets of the Pros." Money, Matter, and More Musings. Last modified October 10, 2011. https://www. taoofmakingmoney.com.

Gardner, Howard. *Creating Minds – An Anatomy of Creativity*. New York: Basic Books, 1993.

Garvin, David. "Is Yours a Learning Organization?" *Harvard Business Review* (March 2008): 109–116.

Gelb, Michael. *Discover Your Genius*. New York: First Quill, 2003.

Gelb, Michael J. *How to Think Like Leonardo da Vinci – Seven Steps to Genius Every Day*. Hamburg: Delta Trade Paperbacks, 1998.

Gerzon, Mark. "Moving Beyond Debate: Start a Dialogue." *Harvard Business School Working Knowledge* (May 22, 2006).

Gilkey, Roderick and Kilts, Clint. "Cognitive Fitness." *Harvard Business Review* (November 2007): 53–60.

Gino, F. and Ariely, D. "The Dark Side of Creativity: Original Thinkers Can Be More Dishonest." Harvard Business School Working Paper 11-064 (February 2011).

Gottman, John M. "Making Relationships Work." *Harvard Business Review* (December 2007): 45–50.

Gourville, John T. "The Curse of Innovation: A Theory of Why Innovative New Products Fail in the Marketplace." *Harvard Business School Marketing Research Paper No. 05-06* (2006).

Green, Jay. "Reinventing Corporate R&D." *BusinessWeek* (September 22, 2003): 74–76.

Groopman, Jerome. "A Doctor's Rx for CEO Decisionmakers." *Harvard Business Review* (February 2008): 19–20.

Guber, Peter. "The Four Truths of the Storyteller." *Harvard Business Review* (December 2007): 53–59.

Guimera, Roger. "Team Assembly Mechanisms Determine Collaboration Network Structure and Team Performance." *Science*, Vol. 308 (April 29, 2005): 697–702.

"Habits for Long-Term Good Brain Health." *Guardian Health Newsletter* (January 2010).

Halverson, H.G. "Nine Things Successful People Do Differently." HBR Blog Network, Last updated February 25, 2011. http:/blogs.hbr.org/cs/2011/02/nine_things_successful_people.html.

Hamel, Gary. "Best Way to Lead Innovation? Learn From Positive Deviants and Challenge Truths." *Optimize* (January 2007).

Hammond, J., Keeney, R., and Raiffa, H. *Smart Choices*. Boston: Harvard Business School Press, 1999.

Hanna, Julia. "Getting Down to the Business of Creativity." *Harvard Business School Working Knowledge Newsletter* (May 2008).

Harris, Kathy. "Case Study: SAIC Innovates From Success." *Gartner Research*, ID Number: G00147822 (March 23, 2007).

Harvey, Jerry B. "The Abilene Paradox and other Meditations on Management". *Organizational Dynamics* 3, 1 (Summer 1974).

Heath, Chip and Heath, Dan. *Made to Stick – Why Some Ideas Survive and Others Die.* New York: Random House, 2007.

Heskett, Jim. "Is the 'Innovator's Solution' to Sustained Corporate Growth an Unnatural Act?" *Harvard Business School Working Knowledge Newsletter* (October 6, 2003).

Hirshberg, Jerry. *The Creative Priority. New York:* Harper Business, 1998.

Hon, Aron. Commented related during a NRO innovation forum discussion. August 2009.

Horowitz, Roni. Advanced Systematic Innovation Techniques (ASIT), On-Line Support Manual. Last modified February 1, 2011. http://start2think.com.

"Innovation Measurement: Tracking the State of Innovation in the American Economy." A Report to the US Secretary of Commerce by the Advisory Committee on Measuring Innovation in the 21st Century Economy. Last modified January 2008. http://www.kauffman.org.

"Intense Exercise May Protect Aging Brain." *USA Today*, Last updated June 9, 2011. www.intelihealth.com.

Isaacs, William. *Dialogue: The Art of Thinking Together.* Boston: Crown Business, 1999.

Johnson, Lauren Keller. "Four Practices for Great Performance." *Harvard Business School Working Knowledge Newsletter* (August 23, 2004).

Kaku, M. *Einstein's Cosmos.* New York: W.W. Norton Company, 2004.

Kamenetz, Anya. "Exercising Mind's Muscle." *Fast Company* (June 2011): 56–59.

Kirton, M.J. *Adaptors and Innovators: Styles of Creativity and Problem-Solving.* London: Routledge, 1994.

Livingston, Gordon. *Too Soon Old, Too Late Smart.* New York: Marlowe & Company, 2004.

Lugaris, Paolo. "Father of Invention: Paolo Lugari's 7 Secrets for Creating Creativity." *Business 2.0* (October 2007).

Mann, Darrell and DeWulf, Simon. "Updating TRIZ: 1985-2002 Patent Research Findings." (CREAX nv, Belgium), TRIZCON2003: 5th Annual International Conference of Altshuller Institute for TRIZ Studies, held at Philadelphia, PA, USA, on March 16–18, 2003.

Maslow, A.H. "A Theory of Human Motivation." *Psychological Review* 50(4) (1943):370–96.

Mauboussin, Michael J. "What Good Are Experts?" *Harvard Business Review* (February 2008).

McCullough, David. "Timeless Leadership: A Conversation with David McCullough." *Harvard Business Review* (March 2008):45–49.

McGee, Marianne. "Innovation Marketplace Helps People With Good Ideas Find Problems." Last modified April 26 2008. *http://www.informationweek.com/story/showArticle.jhtml?articleID=207401938.*

McGregor, Jena. "Big Pharma Makes Nice." *Business Week* (April 24, 2006): 63–76.

McGoff, Chris. *The Primes – How Any Group Can Solve Any Problem*. New York: The Clearing, Inc., 2011.

McKnight, D. and Pletka, R. *Soccer is a Thinking Game*. New York: iUniverse, 2009.

McKnight, D. "The National Space Policy: High Tech Requires High Touch." *High Frontier* (February 2011): 73–77.

Medina, John. "The Board Meeting of the Future." *Harvard Business Review* (February 2008): 22–23.

Miller, George. "The Magical Number Seven, Plus or Minus Two: Some Limits on Our Capacity for Processing Information." *Psychological Review, vol. 63* (1956): 81–97.

Nalebuff, Barry and Ayres, Ian. "Einstein You're Not – and Don't Have To Be." *Harvard Business School Working Knowledge Newsletter* (November 3, 2003).

National Research Council. "Limiting Future Collision Risk to Spacecraft – An Assessment of NASA's Meteoroid and Orbital Debris programs." Washington, DC: The National Academies Press, Washington, 2011.

Nisbett, R. E. *The Geography of Thought*. New York: Free Press, 2003.

Nohria, N., Groysberg, B., and Lee, L-E. "Employee Motivation." *Harvard Business Review* (July–August 2008): 78–82.

O'Connell, Andrew. "Hotter Heads Prevail." *Harvard Business Review* (December 2007): 22.

Page, Scott E. *The Difference*. Princeton: Princeton University Press, 2007.

Parsons, P. *3-Minute Einstein*. New York: Metro Books, 2011.

Patterson, K., Grenny, J., McMillan, R., and Switzler, A. *Crucial Conversations*, New York: McGraw-Hill, 2002.

Pike, Daniel. *A Whole New Mind*. New York: The Berkeley Publishing Group, 2006.

Robbins, Stever. "Tips for Mastering E-Mail Overload." *Harvard Business School Working Knowledge Newsletter* (November 1, 2004).

Roberts, Michael. "The Power of Ordinary Practices." *Harvard Business School Working Knowledge Newsletter* (September 20, 2006).

Rogers, Carl R. and Roethsliberger, F.J. "Barriers and Gateways to Communication." *Harvard Business Review*, No. 91610 (1991).

Seybold, Patricia. "Customer-Controlled Innovation." *Optimize* (February 2007): 27–31.

Shapiro, Stephen. "Why Statistics Kill Innovation." Innovation Tools Web Site, Last updated April 2008. www.innovationtools.com.

Schrage, Michael. "Much Ado About Innovation." *MIT Technology Review* (May 2004): 17.

Seely, John and Thomas, Douglas. "The Gamer Disposition." *Harvard Business Review* (February 2008).

Sengupta, Kishore. "The Experience Trap." *Harvard Business Review* (February 2008).

Senor, Dan and Singer, Saul. *Start-Up Nation: The Story of Israel's Economic Miracle*. New York: 12 Twelve, 2009.

Silverthorne, Sean. "Understanding Users of Social Networks." *Harvard Business School Working Knowledge Newsletter* (September 14, 2009).

Sheldrake, Rupert. *The Presence of the Past*. New York: Times Books, 1988.

Sloane, Patrick. "What Not To Do: Six Ways to Ruin a Brainstorming Session." Last updated April, 2008. www.RealInnovation.com.

Snowden, David J. and Boone, Mary E. "A Leader's Framework for Decision Making." *Harvard Business Review* (November 2007): 68-74.

Sobel, Dava. *Longitude*. New York: Penguin Books, 1995.

Stadler, Christian. "The Four Principles of Enduring Success." *Harvard Business Review* (July–August 2007): 62-72.

Stiller, J. "Exploit What You Do Best." *Harvard Management Update*, Vol. 8, No. 8 (August 2003).

Strauch, Barbara. *The Secret Life of the Grown-Up Brain: The Surprising Talents of the Middle-Aged Brain*. New York: Viking Press, 2010.

Sykes, Charles. *Dumbing Down Our Kids*. New York: St Martin's Griffin, 1996.

Templeton, Brad. *"10 Big Myths About Copyright Explained."* Last updated June 2004. www.templetons.com/bard/copymyths.

"The Innovator's Advantage." *On-Call Research Report for Ashland-Valvoline*, ILO Institute (February 7, 2007).

Thomke, Stefan. *Experimentation Matters*. Boston: Harvard Business School Press, 2003.

Tost, L.P., Gino, F., and Larrick, R. P. "When power makes others speechless: The negative impact of leader power on team performance." Harvard Business School Working Paper 11-087 (2011).

Tucker, Robert B. *Driving Growth Through Innovation*. San Francisco: B-K Publishers, Inc., 2002.

Turner, G. *North Pole, South Pole*. New York: The Experiment, 2011.

Twain, Mark. *Innocents Abroad*. Last updated June 7, 2007. www.mtwain.com.

Von Oech, Roger. *Expect the Unexpected or You Won't Find It*. New York: Free Press, 2001.

"Want Better Memory." *Men's Health* (November 2005): 32-34.

Wasserstein, Bruce. "Giving Great Advice." *Harvard Business Review* (February 2008): 106-110.

Wolff, Michael. "Forget R&D Spending – Think Innovation." *Research Technology Management* (March–April 2007).

Wooden, J. and Jamison, S. *Wooden*. New York: McGraw-Hill, 1997.

Wootley, J. "A Clear Eye For Innovation." *Harvard Business School Working Knowledge Newsletter* (April 26, 2004).

Wujec, Tom. "Design Fundamentals." *MIT Technology Review* (April 1, 2011).

Crossword Puzzle Solution

www.Puzzle-Maker.com